Celebration Carvings

Ron Ransom

Text written with and photography by Dawn Stoltzfus

Schiffer Publishing Ltd

4880 Lower Valley Road, Atglen, PA 19310 USA

To the "Lively" Twelve—Betty and Bob, Fred and Ethelyn, John and Betty, Harvey and Rachel, Bobby and Virginia, and, of course, Evelyn and me.

After God and family, to most of us, our friends are special. Evelyn and I have known the friends to whom I dedicated this book since elementary school days. We have spent many special days together celebrating the births of our children and grandchildren and grieving family deaths. Although we are not as "lively" as we once were, we still love, laugh, and eat as much as ever.

Library of Congress Catalog Card Number: 97-68171

Book Design by: Laurie A. Smucker

ISBN: 0-7643-0362-7
Printed in China

Published by Schiffer Publishing Ltd.
4880 Lower Valley Road
Atglen, PA 19310
Phone: (610) 593-1777; Fax: (610) 593-2002
E-mail: schifferbk@aol.com
Please write for a free catalog.
This book may be purchased from the publisher.
Please include $3.95 for shipping.
Try your bookstore first.

We are interested in hearing from authors with book ideas on related subjects.

Contents

Foreword

For more years than both of us are reluctant to admit, Ron Ransom and I have worked together at the City of Marietta, Georgia. By the time I came on board there, he was already an institution in Marietta. A dynamic head of the Marietta Parks and Recreation Department, a professional cartoonist, a radio talk-show host, and somehow in all of that, an excellent woodcarver.

In fact, of all his talents he came to be most associated with his woodcarving. All the top-name charities came to him for a signed "Ron Ransom Original" which was sure to bring big dollars to their cause. More and more he was asked to customize carvings for personal gifts and public awards. Sometimes Santas, sometimes angels, sometimes something else.

More and more, too, he was besieged by would-be carvers wanting him to teach a class. And teach he did. Just as he had been generous with sharing his works with charities, Ron was generous—and passionate—about sharing his skills and knowledge. His prowess as a teacher led him to write carving books to reach the broader audience. Ron Ransom is now admired all over the country as he has been in Marietta for decades.

It is appropriate that this newest book, his ninth, is about carving for celebrations. Anyone who knows Ron—and his lovely wife Evelyn—know they celebrate life every day. Always the favorite employee at Marietta City Hall, Ron still comes around to share a few jokes, a lot of smiles, and inevitably brings a gift of some kind for somebody. He celebrates life by giving and sharing. Even in retirement, he is called on by many of us at City Hall for advice, ideas, and inspiration. And he always obliges.

This year Ron became even more dear to me when he coaxed my husband—who has one foot permanently attached to a tennis court somewhere in Atlanta (and has the worn-out knees to prove it)—to attend one of his woodcarving classes. Ron's enthusiasm and encouragement ignited my husband's interest and latent abilities, and now I'm married to a woodcarver as well as a tennis player.

It is just this kind of contagious enthusiasm for life and art that makes Ron Ransom so special. Although I doubt I'll ever pick up a knife or a chunk of wood, my life will be forever changed and blessed because Ron Ransom touched it.

So will yours.

Audrey T. Griffies
Public Information Officer
City of Marietta, Georgia

Introduction

While searching for a title for this book, I asked for suggestions from youngsters at several of the schools were I was demonstrating carving. They continued to come up with a "Holiday" in the title. I explained that with a little stretch of the imagination, that Father Time represents a holiday because it presented a New Year. I hope one or more of the special days is special to you, and you will enjoy giving these carvings a try.

Send your questions or comments to:

Ron Ransom
Box 4101
Marietta, GA 30061

Please enclose a self-addressed, stamped envelope if you want an answer.

Those of you who have used my other books know that I mostly use a knife. Don't be concerned with all the tools shown here. Sometimes they help move some wood, but a knife alone will be fine.

The tools we will be using.

Father Time

When I showed this carving to elementary school kids, some knew what it represented while others called it the Grim Reaper. Father Time has spent a rough year and does look a little beat. With a little imagination, you could also turn this piece into a Father Christmas.

This pattern is reproduced at 80%.
To restore photocopy at 125%.

Father Time, before and after.

With a foredom tool, I roughed this one in a little. As you will see as we move along, it can easily be done with a knife.

Round the back side of the arm which will be holding the scythe.

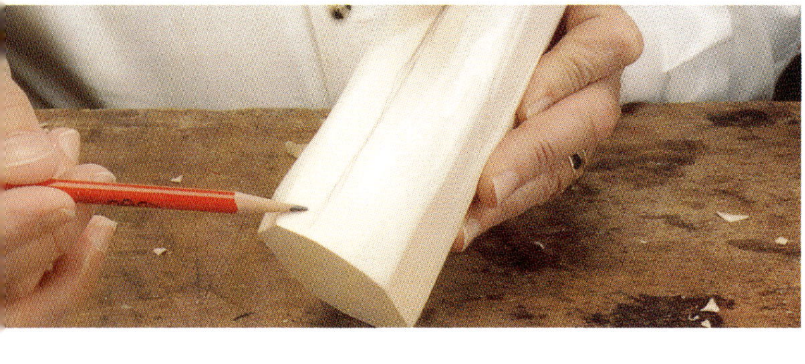

We will start from the back side, drawing a line in the middle to have something to carve towards.

I am making the hair more prominent using the Flexcut tool.

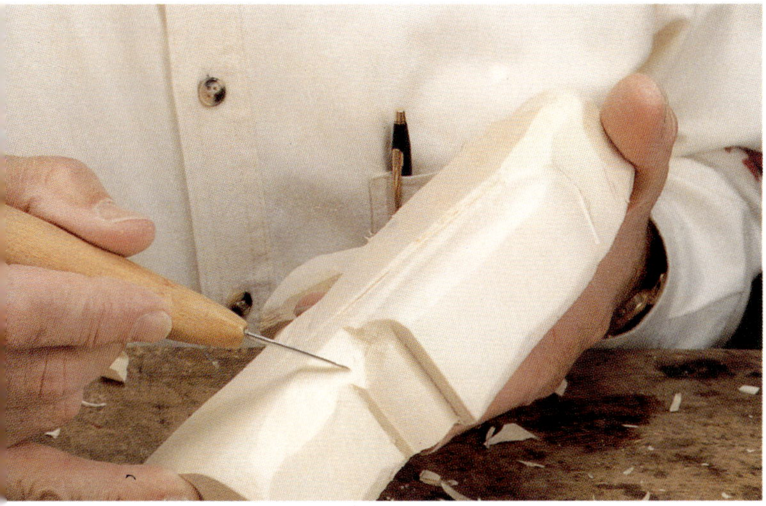

Begin to shape the area where the arm comes along the body.

You can use a fishtail gouge to take out bigger chunks of wood.

Define the back of the arm with the v-Flexcut tool.

Shape the front of the left arm with a flatter Flexcut tool.

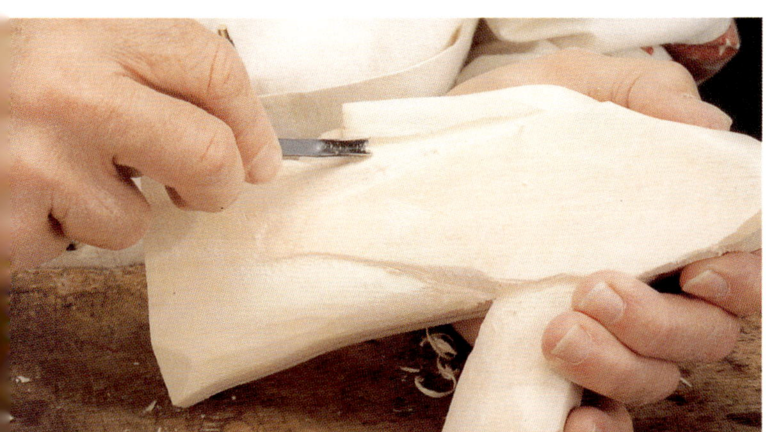

Do the same on the front of the arm.

Work the right shoulder into the beard and hair, using the knife again.

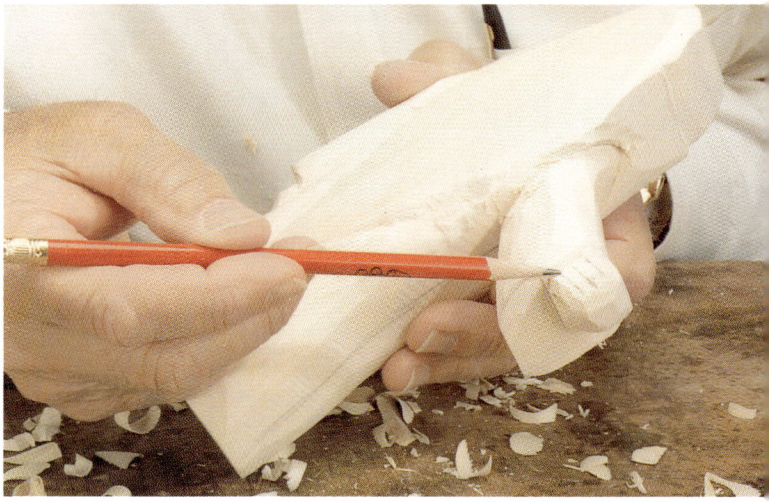

Draw in the fingers on Father Time's hand by first drawing one line down the middle and then filling in the others...

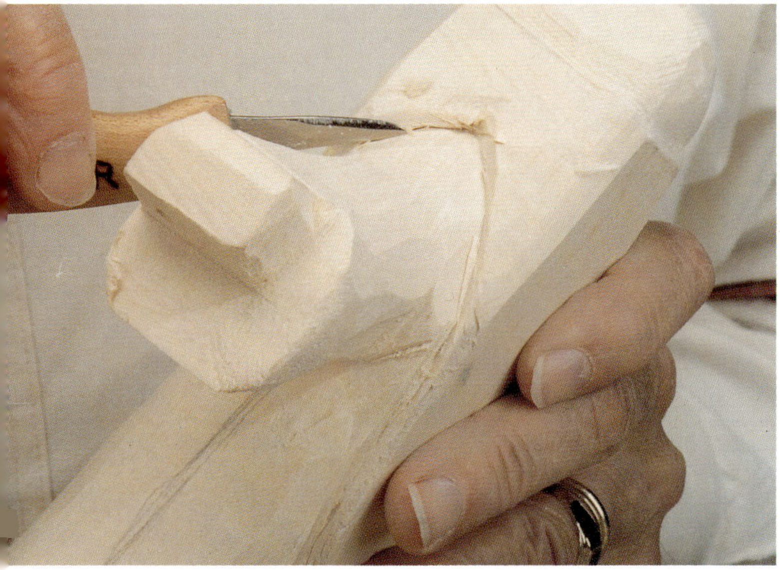

Do the same thing on the other arm.

...and carve them in with the Flexcut tool.

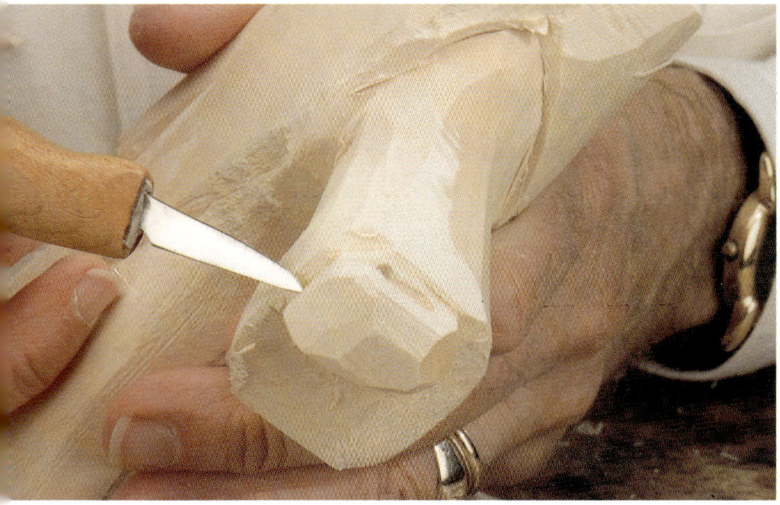

Begin to shape the hand that will hold the scythe.

Draw in the other hand.

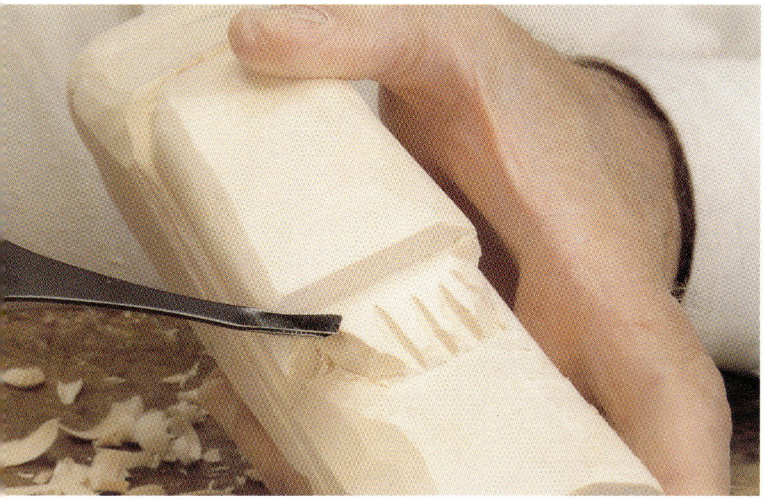

I have cut the fingers out with the gouge tool, and am going to trim them down with the knife because as they are now, they look like a baseball glove.

Define the bald head where it goes into the beard and the head with the v-tool.

The hand is now trimmed down so it looks close to the other hand in size.

Continue to round and take off the rough spots.

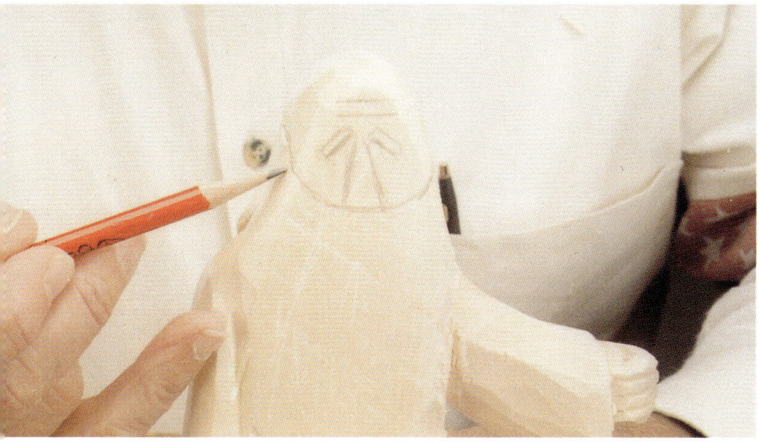

I have drawn in the face so I have some guidelines to follow.

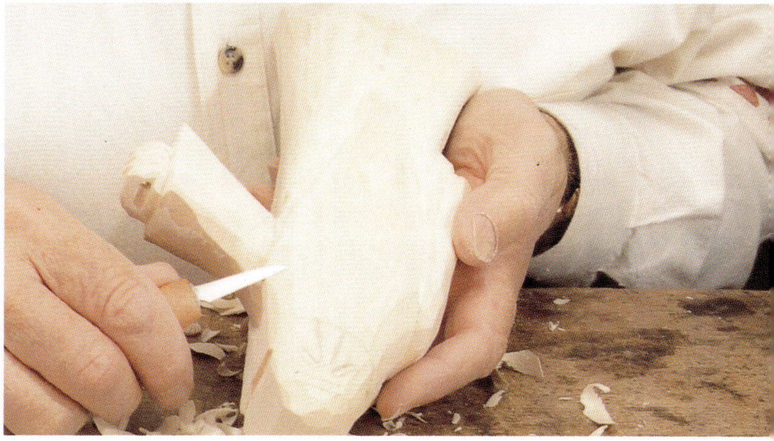

I feel the beard needs to be rounded to give it some definition, so I'm rounding off the edges.

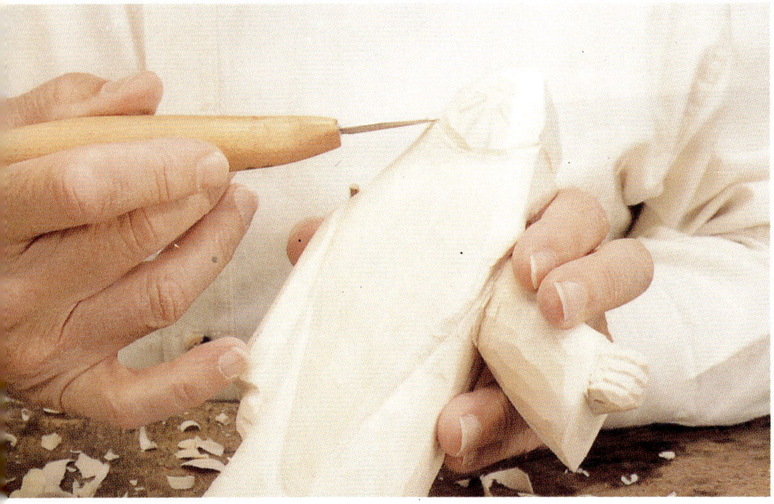

Here I'm starting to shape the egg head, and may cut out where I have drawn in in pencil but this can easily be drawn back.

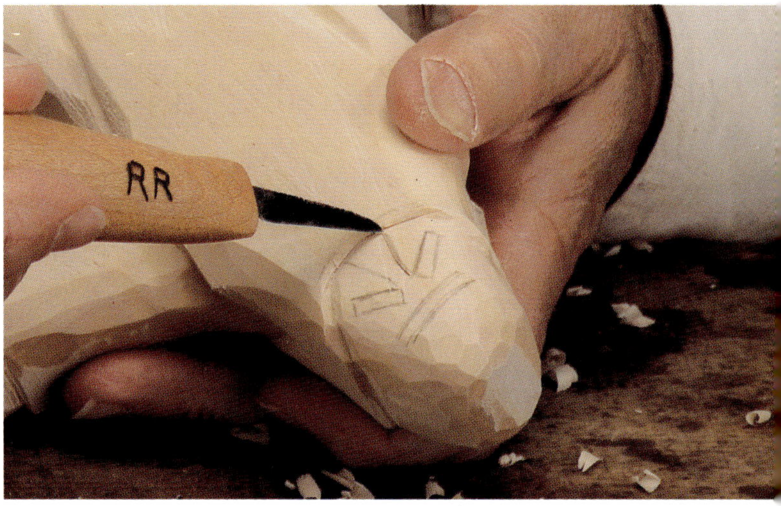

This will be different from a Santa face, because the eye channel as I call it does not come all the way across the face.

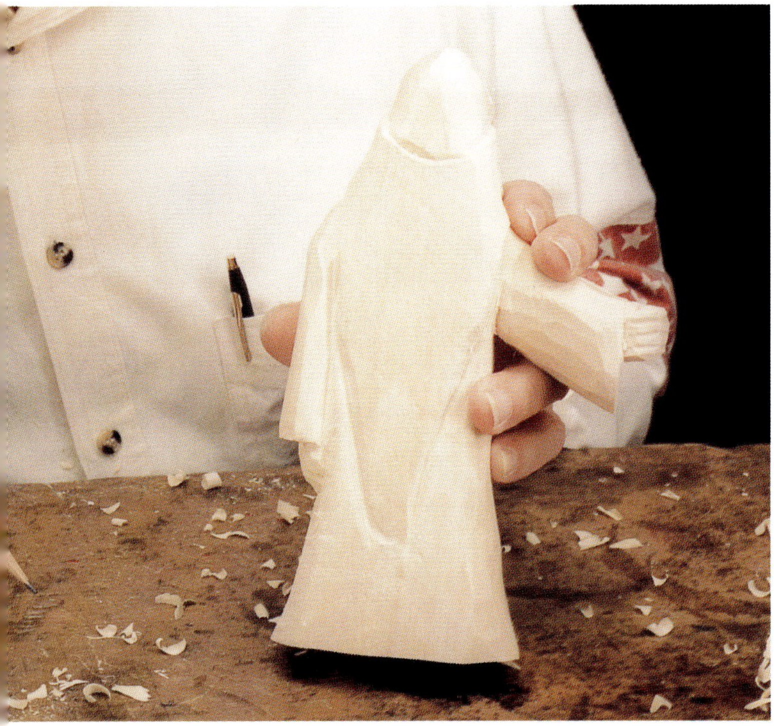

I now have the piece rounded like I wanted, but have to decide which side is front and which is back!

I have drawn my face back in as I want it.

As usual, leave plenty of room for the nose.

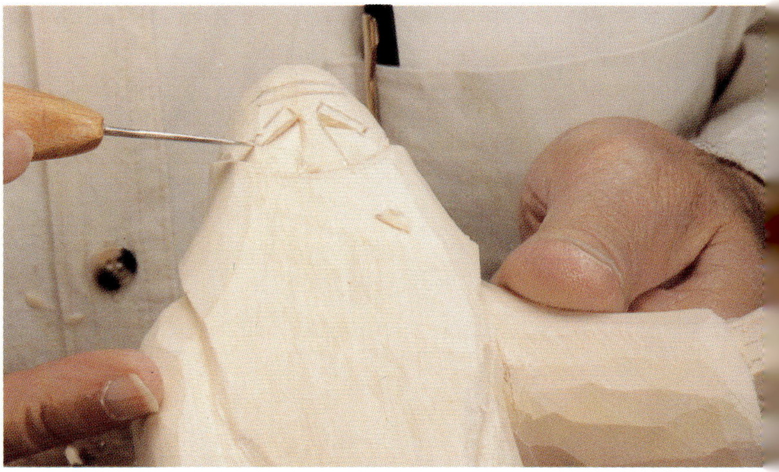

The droopy eyes give him a sad look.

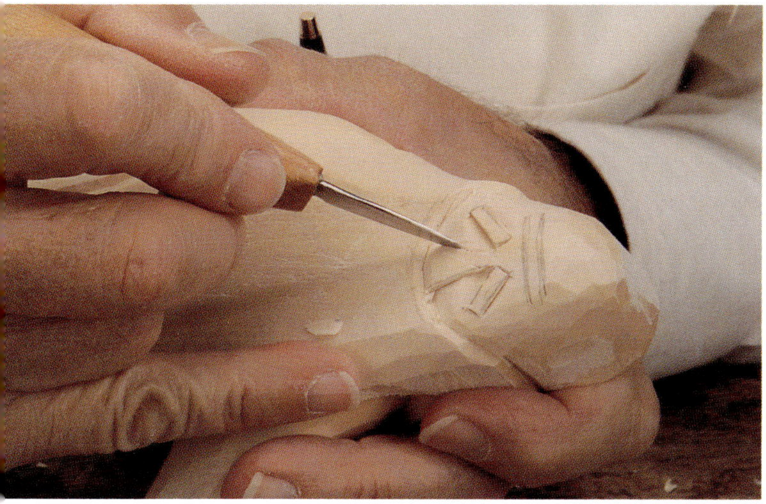

Make a nice deep line on each side of the nose. Shape the nose a little bit more if you like.

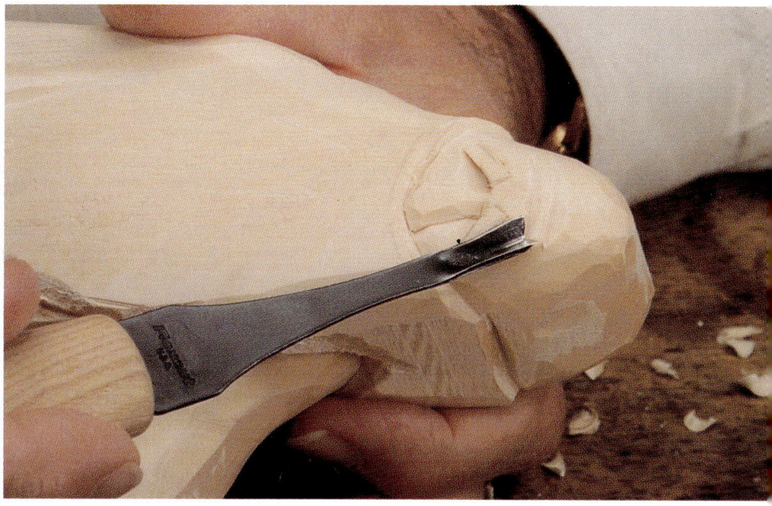

With a v-gouge, carve furrows into the brow.

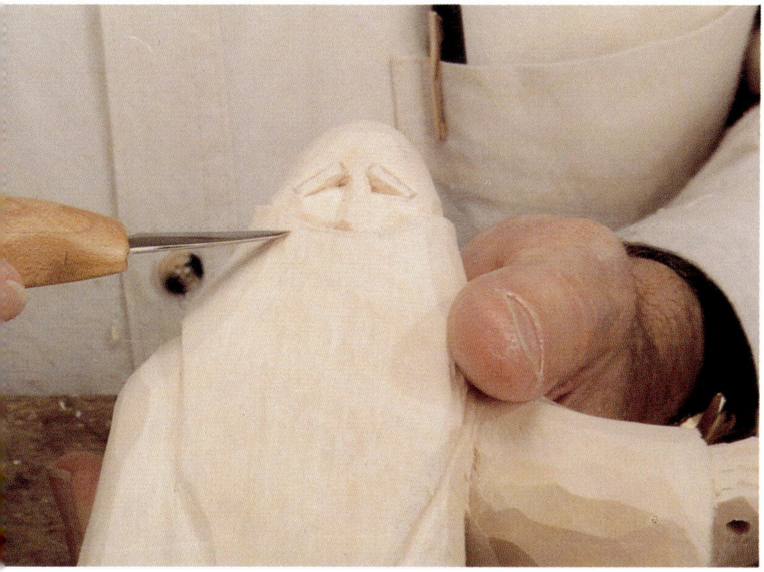

Shape the nose and round the cheeks into the beard.

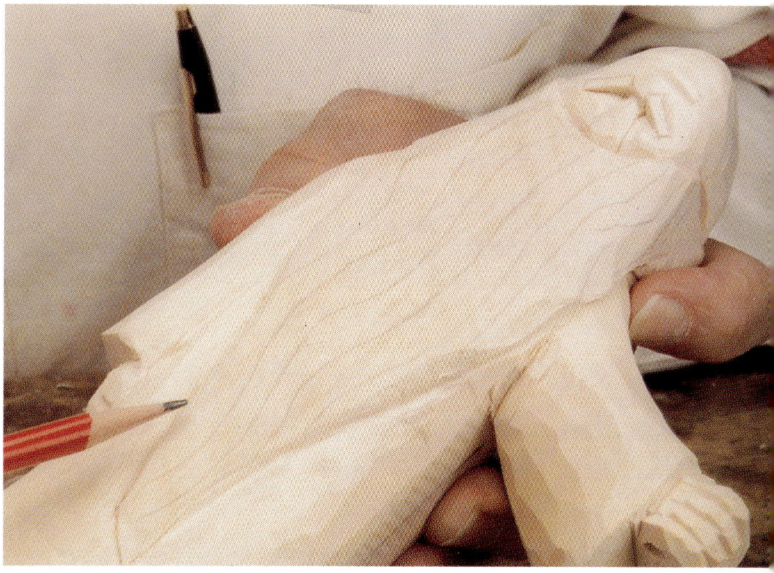

Before you begin to detail the beard, you may want to draw in some lines.

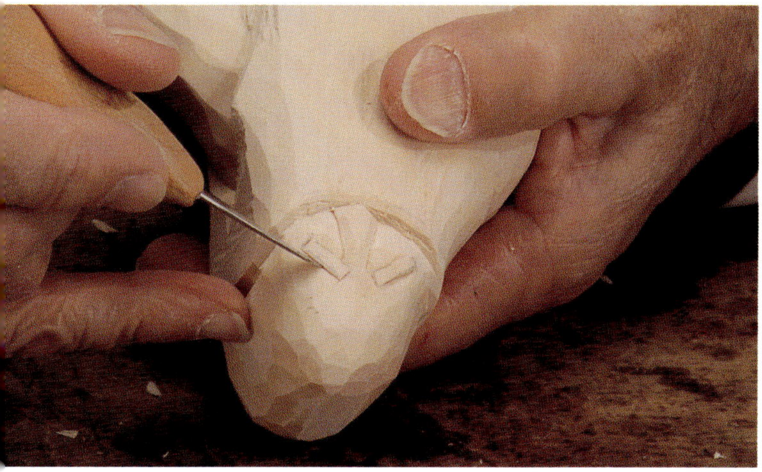

Carefully trim around the eyebrows.

Detailing the beard with a v-tool.

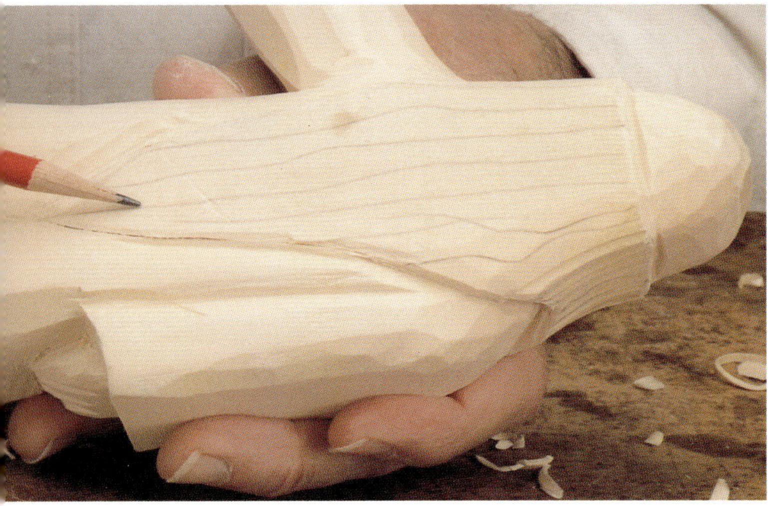

Draw in your lines on the hair in the back.

Using the knife, incise a line along the pencil marks...

...then come back in beside it and make a small strip.

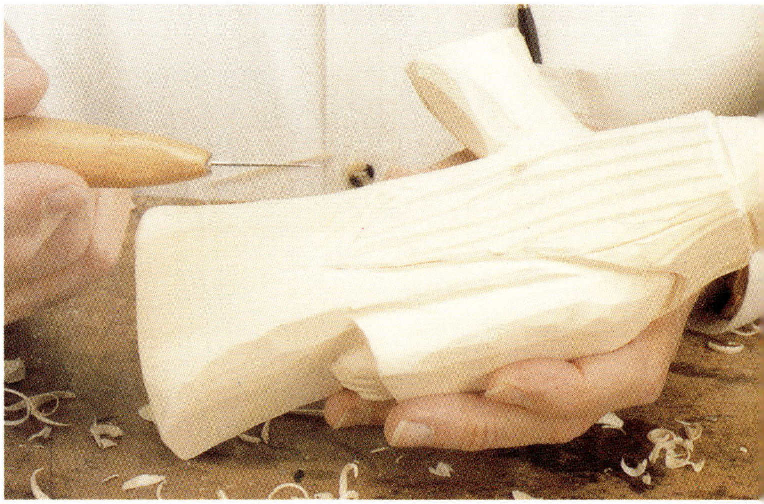

Hair detailing done with the knife.

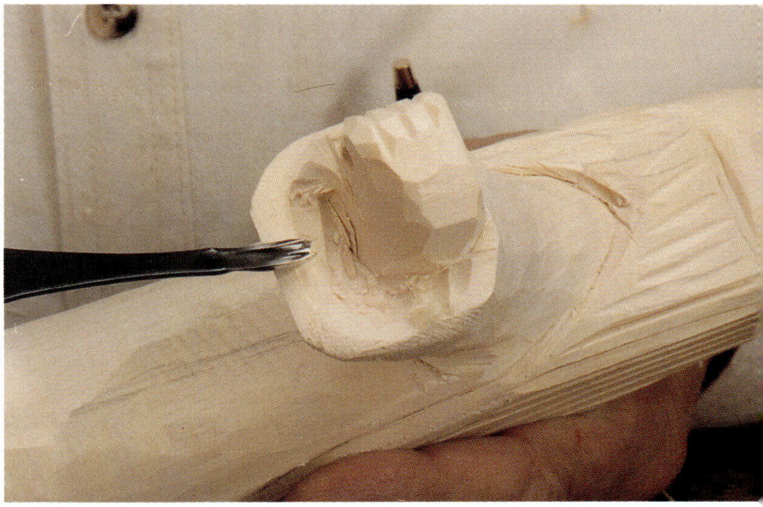

Take the waste from out of the sleeve and under the hand. To do this, I prefer to use the Flexcut tool because of its flexibility.

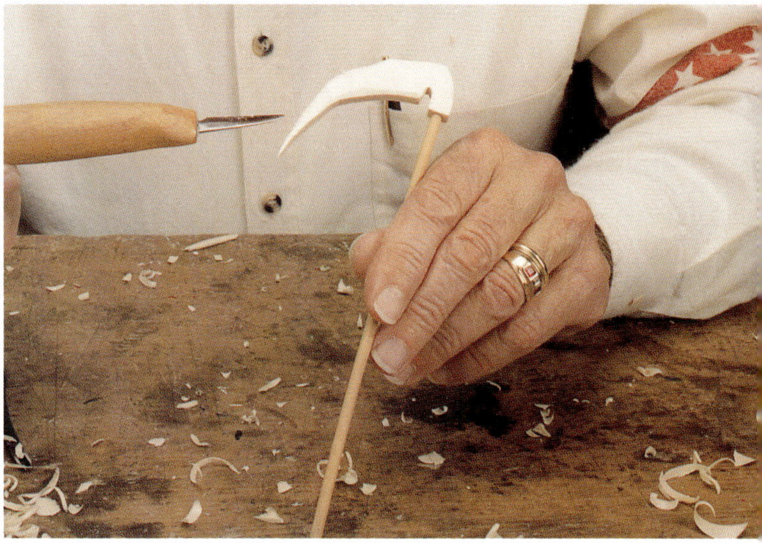

The pattern for the scythe is with the Father Time pattern.

The Leprechaun

I've never been to New York City for a St. Patrick's Day parade, but I have been to one in Savannah, Georgia. For this one day everybody is Irish. If you do not get a tear in your eye when Bing Crosby sings *Too Ra Loo Ra Loo Ra*, you're probably not Irish. I let my friends at the East Cobb Senior Center try this pattern and they were having fun carving it. I guarantee it will bring you good luck if you leave it prominently displayed.

The finished and unfinished leprechaun.

This pattern is reproduced at 80%.
To restore photocopy at 125%.

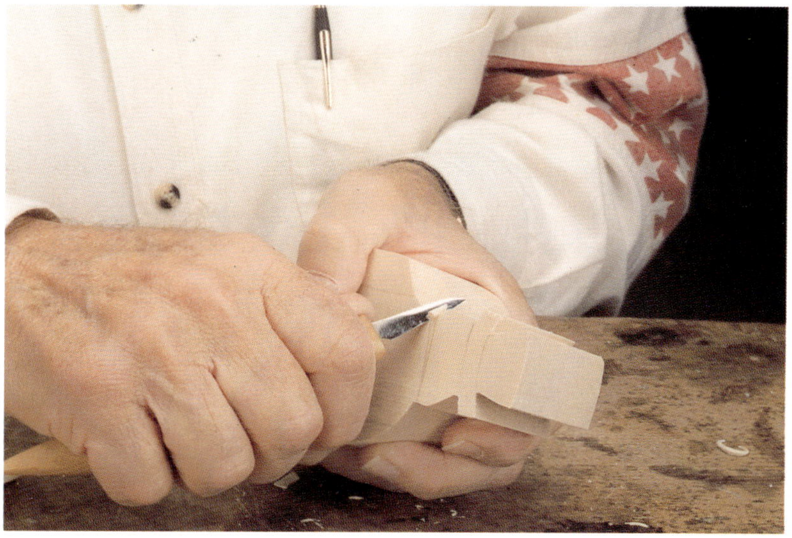

Make a cut between the hair and the left shoulder.

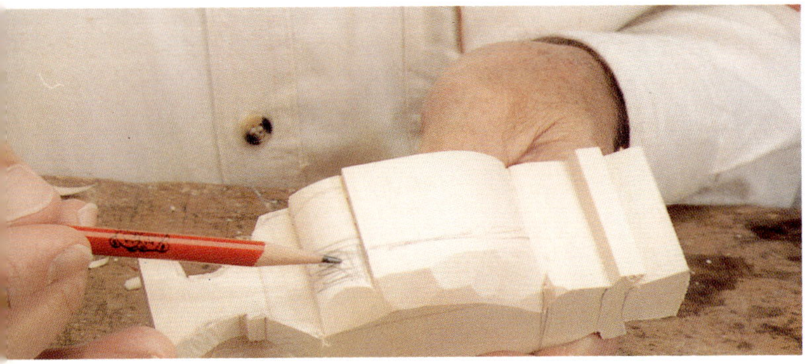

Quite a bit of wood needs to come off here, so I have drawn in the area where I need to cut.

Start to round the shoulders on both sides.

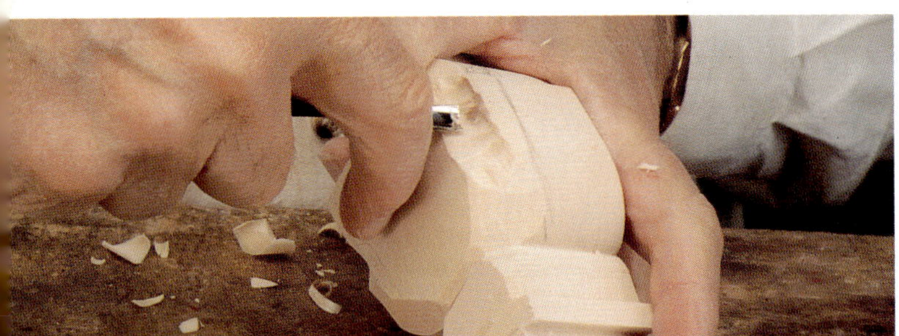

I need to remove a good bit of wood, so I am using the Flexcut gouge here.

The arm is down pretty close to the shape I want it to be.

Begin to round the shoulder on the other side.

Round left shoulder and arm.

Incise and remove a strip of wood between the arm and the body.

PLACE
STAMP
HERE

SCHIFFER PUBLISHING LTD
4880 LOWER VALLEY ROAD
ATGLEN, PA 19310-9717

Cut under right arm to begin defining it.

I have incised the lines for the coat, lapels, hands, and the vest.

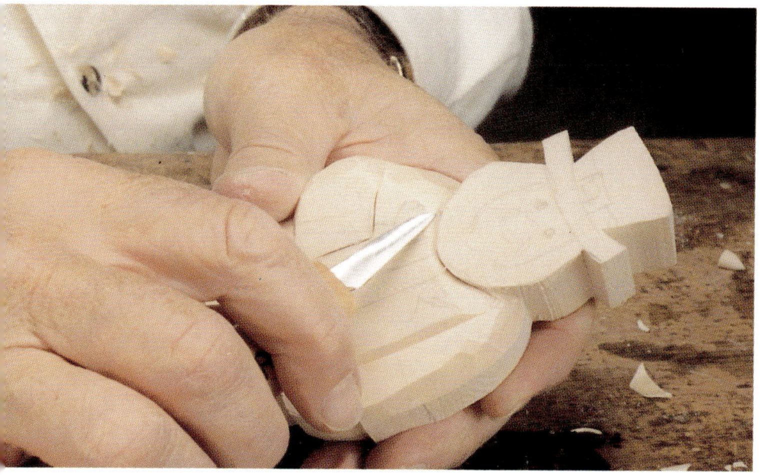

Begin to separate the beard from the rest of the body.

Cut away to start to give the hand and coat definition.

Use a v-gouge to separate the coat from the trousers.

Pick out the small area behind the right arm with the v-gouge.

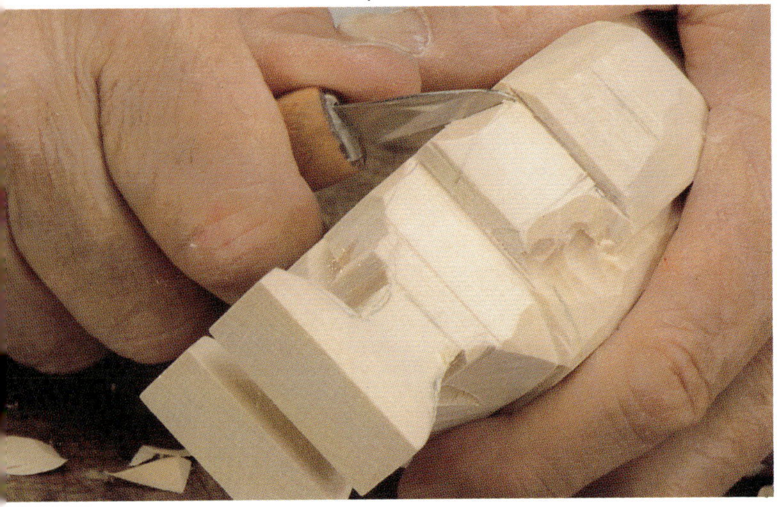

I am beginning to cut the left hand down, trying to match the size of other hand.

Smooth in areas of saw marks on the legs and stockings.

Cut the trouser leg up to the bottom of the shirt.

Gouges are good for getting into small areas.

I have cleaned out this area.

Just round off the shoes, and leave them pretty clunky because we will paint in a buckle.

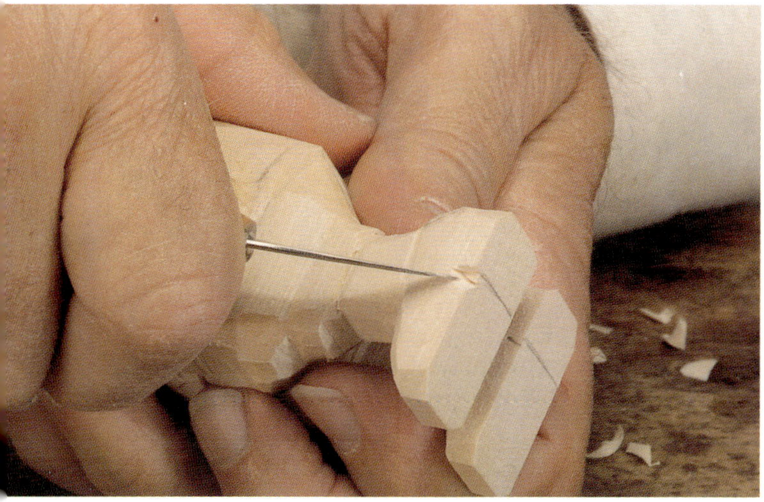

Cut a little notch in the heel on all four sides of the shoe.

Make a definite cut at the top of the brim...

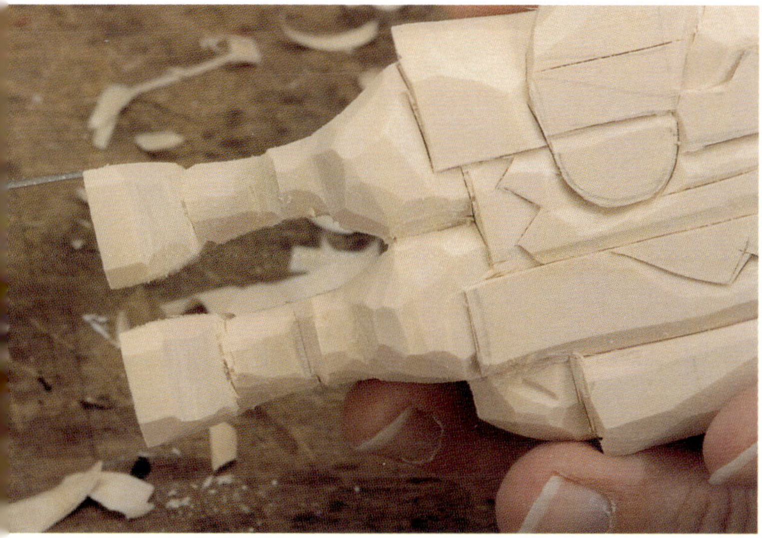

The legs are just about finished, but I may sand them a little bit later.

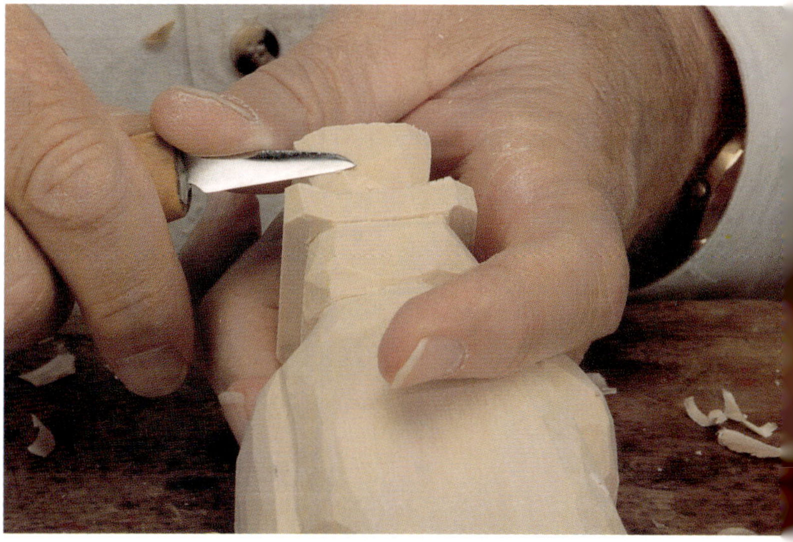

...on both sides of the hat.

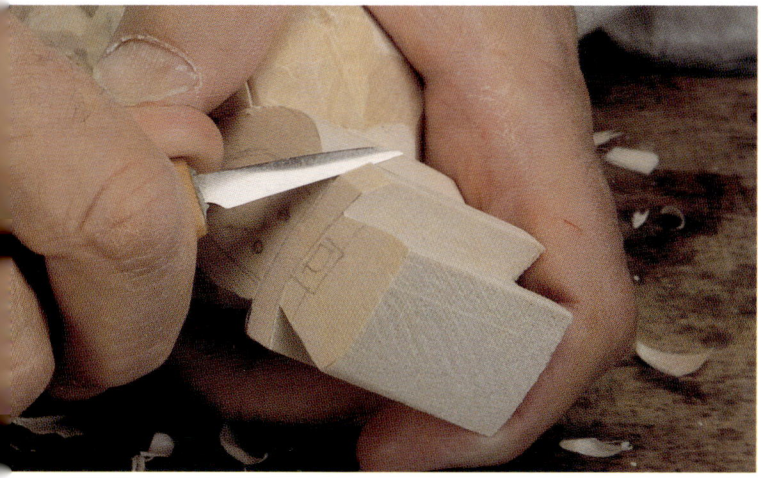

Start rounding the hat.

Round until you get the shape of hat that you want.

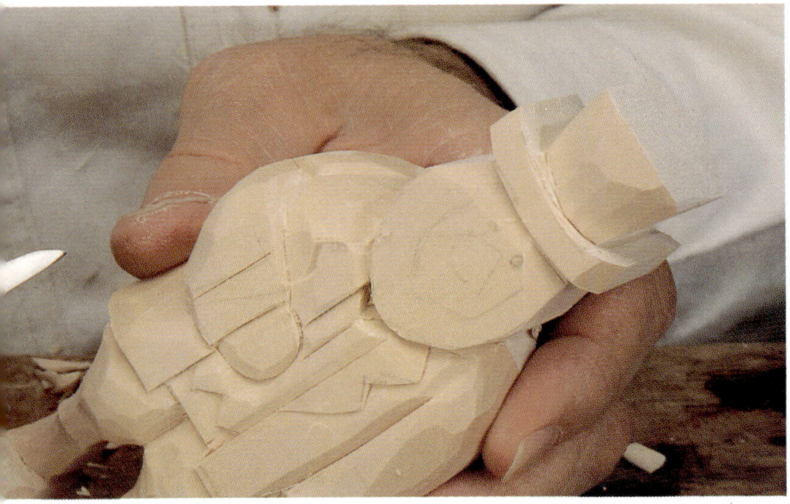

I have begun to define the head, underneath the hat.

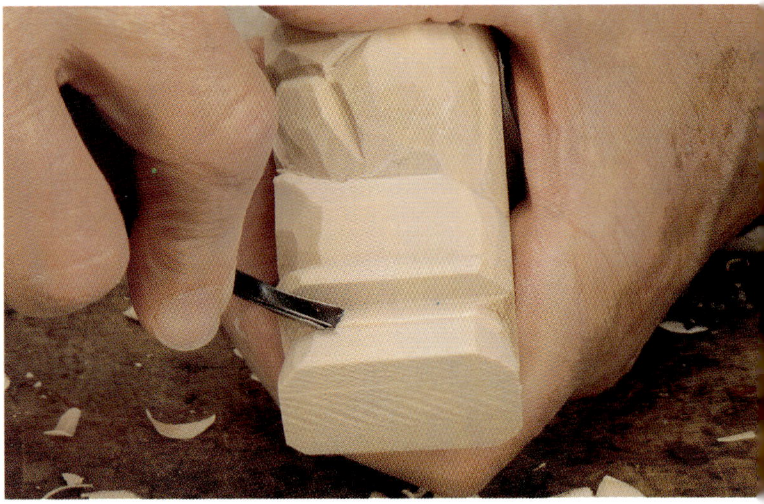

Put in the hat band with the v-gouge.

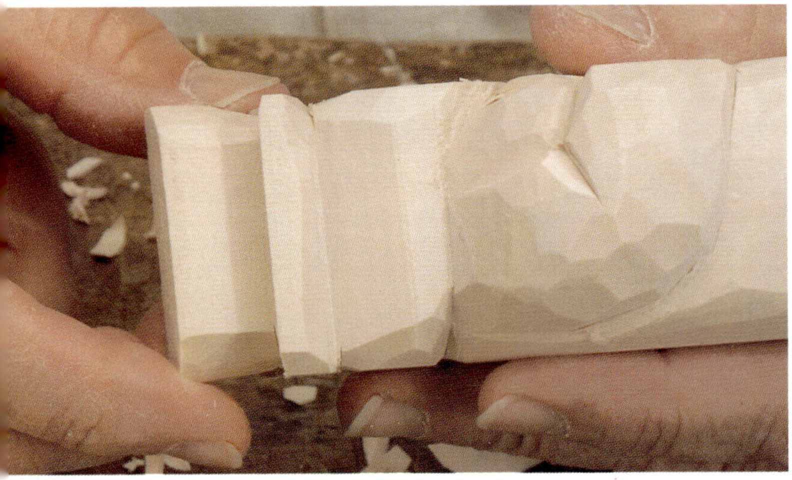

When doing this, I noticed that the brim of the hat needed thinning.

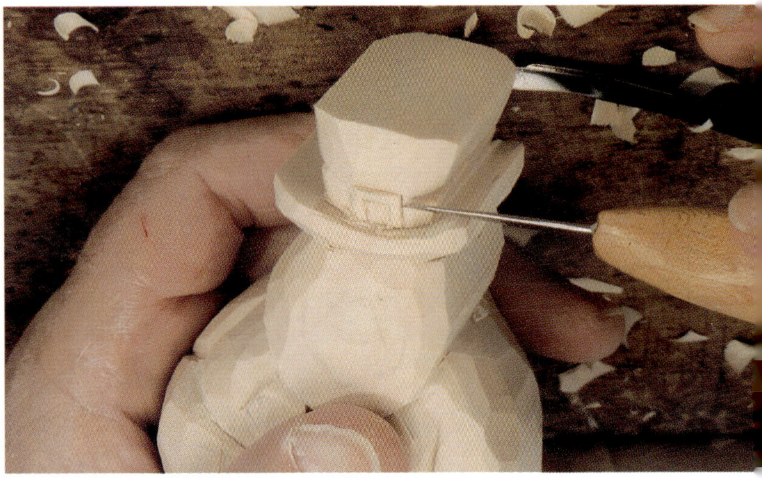

Carve in the buckle on the hat.

Add a hat band and buckle.

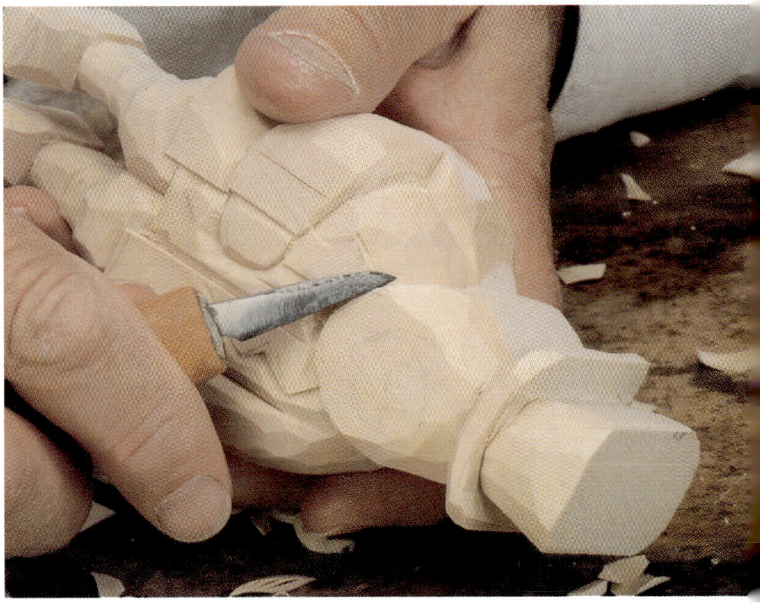

Now round the face.

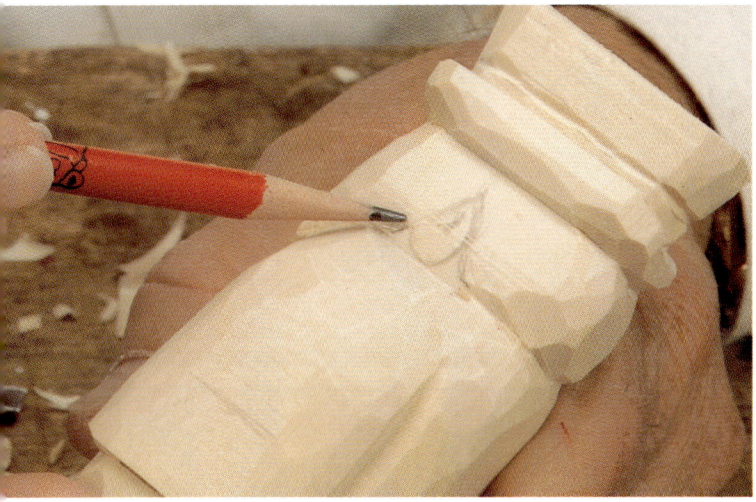

Draw in the ear on each side of the head.

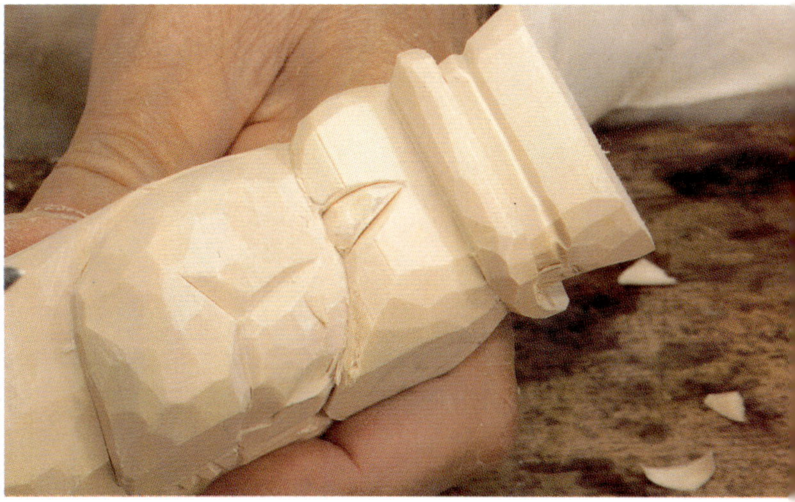

Do a similar ear on the other side of the head.

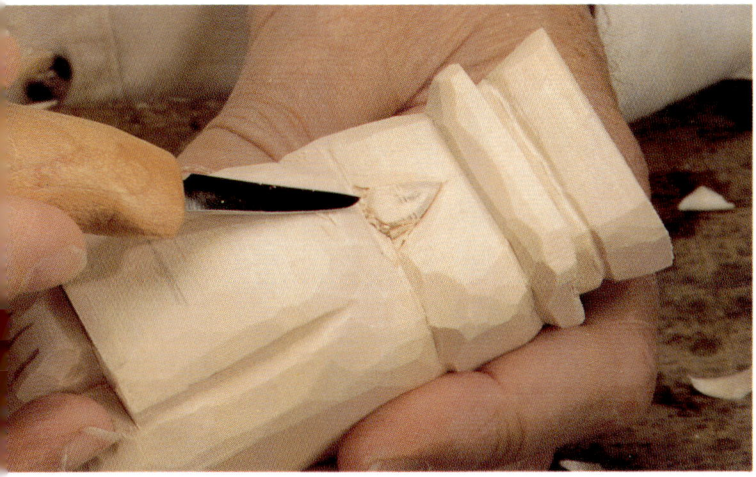

I have roughed out the shape of the ear by cutting away from each side of it.

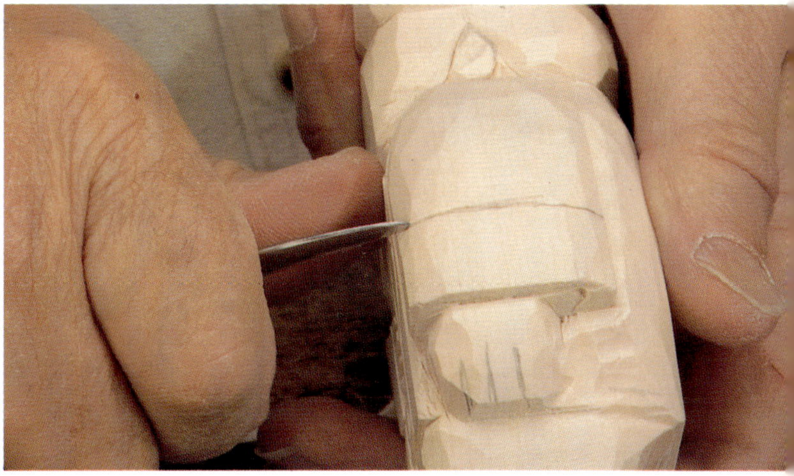

Make a cuff on the sleeve.

Take the gouge and make a small indentation to make it look like an ear.

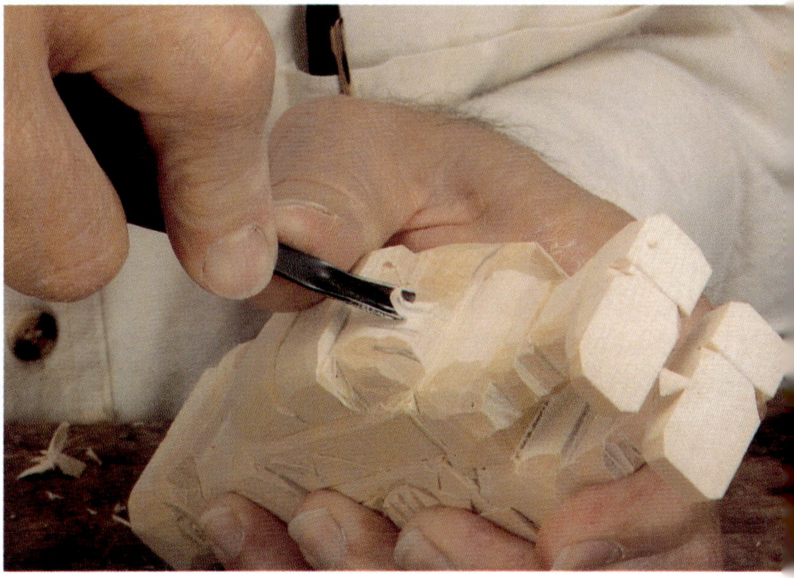

Add the fingers on the left hand with the gouge.

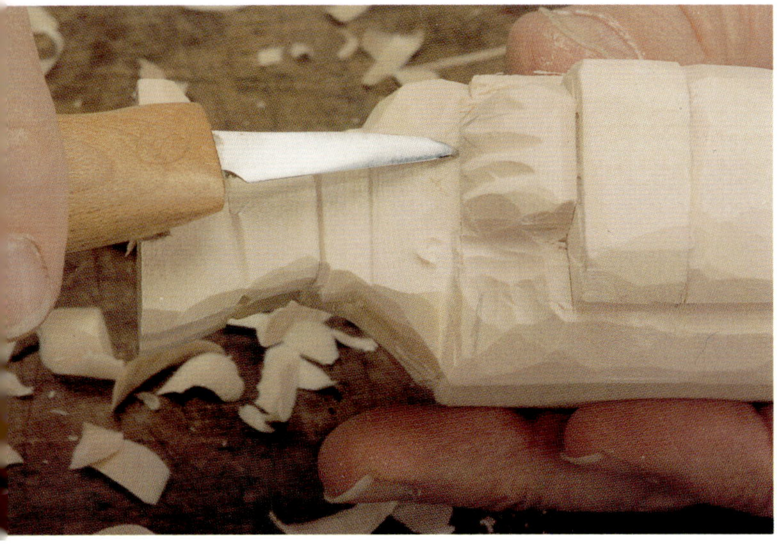

With a manicure, the hand will be ready to paint.

Also add fingers on the right hand with the gouge.

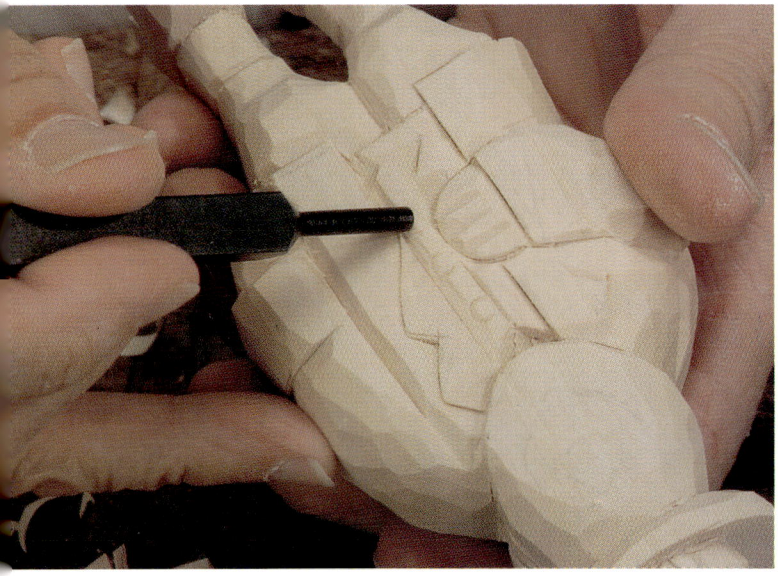

Add buttons on vest and sleeve with the eye punch.

We will now start on the face. I have the basic egg shape, and have drawn in the wide nose and the eyes and cheeks.

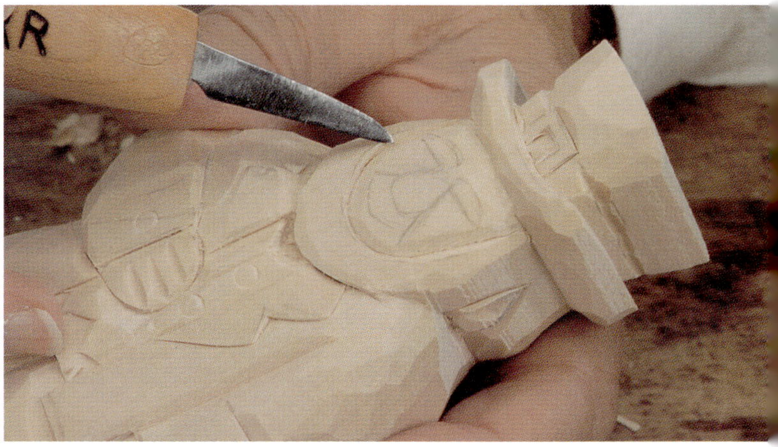

Cut away between the face and the beard.

Incise around the nose.

At this point you should have the cheeks going into the eye area.

Carve smile lines beside the nose.

Soften the line between the beard and the face by rounding it.

Give him some round, happy cheeks.

Carefully trim away fluffy eyebrows.

Cut in a little smiley face if you want your leprechaun to be happy. Check for rough places, and you'll have your lucky leprechaun ready to paint!

Flying Witch

As far back as I can remember (sounds like a good country song title) I have always enjoyed Halloween.

When I was a youngster we didn't do Trick or Treat. We would occasionally play some small prank on someone, such as pushing over an outhouse or writing on store windows with soap. The most fun we had was at our elementary school carnivals where there were booths set up and you could win wonderful prizes. (Remember the little cricket gizmos that you drove your brothers and sisters nuts with?) The cake walk was always a part of the carnival and the spook house was really scary when the resident ghost would hand you a cold eyeball to hold in the dark.

This pattern is reproduced at 80%.
To restore photocopy at 125%.

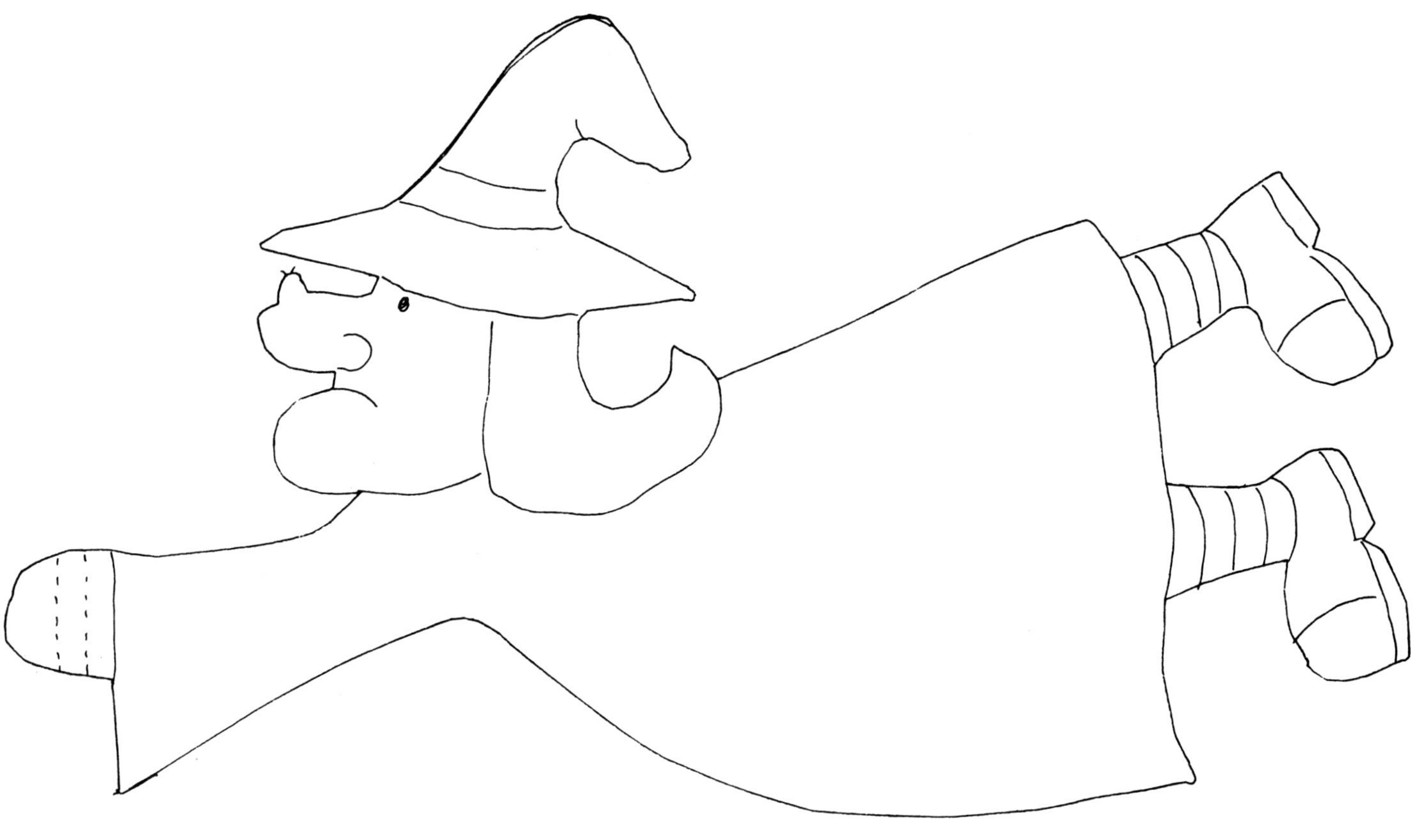

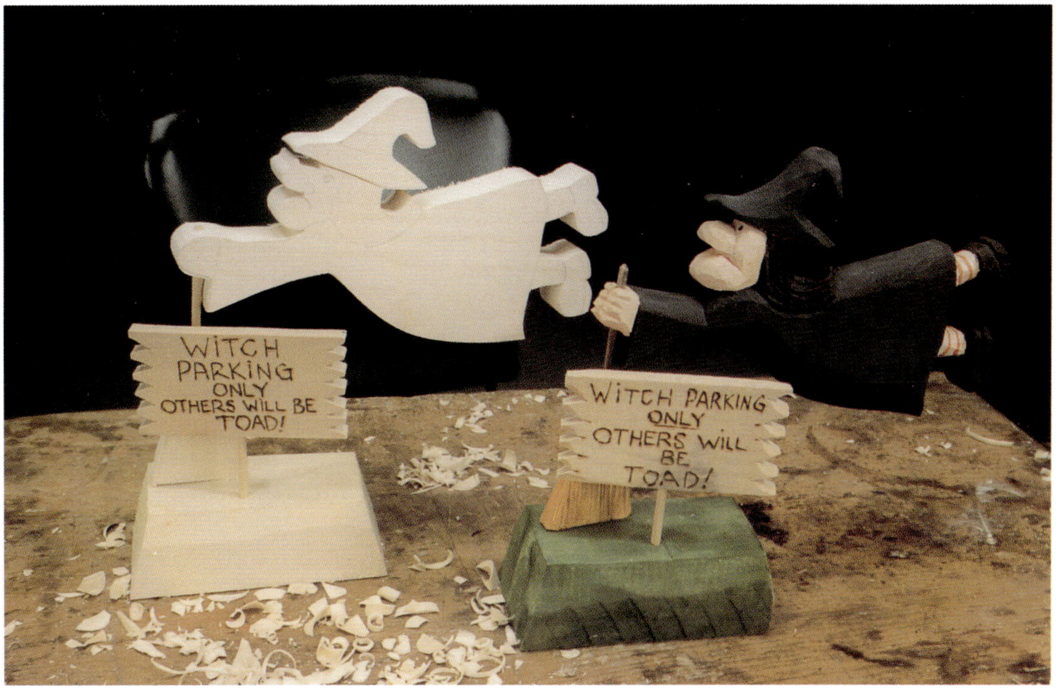

The flying witch, before and after.

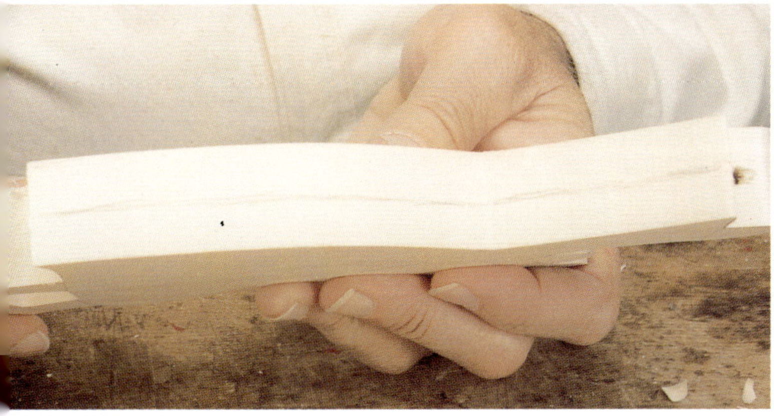

I have found it useful to draw a center line when doing the thinner work to have something to work to.

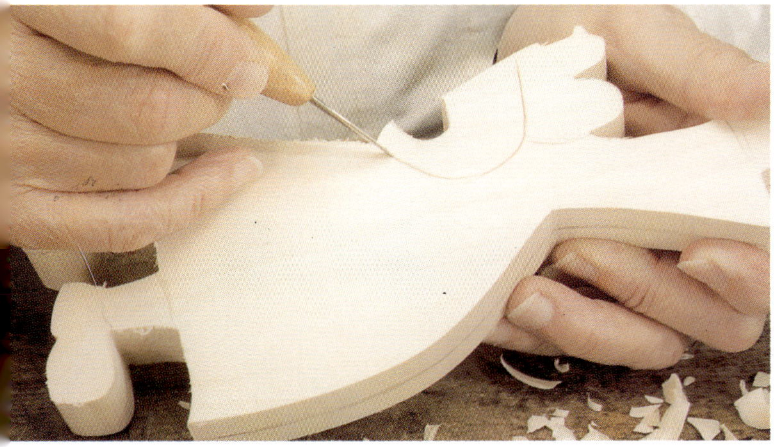

Incise the lines on both sides.

You'll notice I have cut the hat away from the head, and plan to glue or epoxy it back on when I am finished carving. My friend Al Streetman demonstrated this technique on one of his Uncle Sams in one of his Schiffer books. Having the hat out of the way makes it much easier to work on the face.

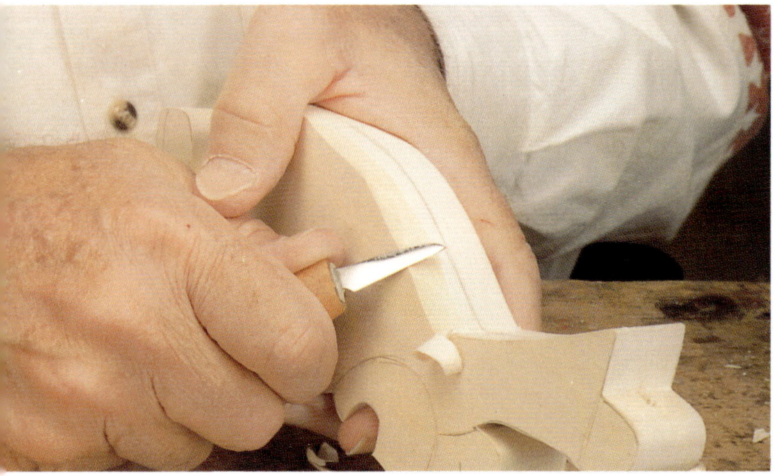

Round the bottom of the ridge.

Do this on both sides, toward the center line.

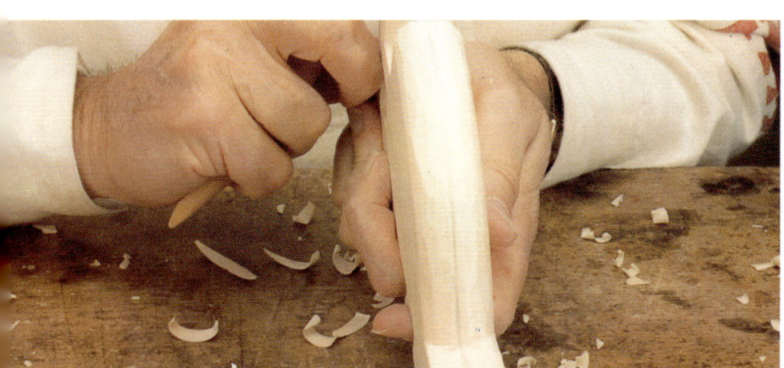

The bottom of witch's dress—notice the line is still there.

Now I will round the arms toward the center line.

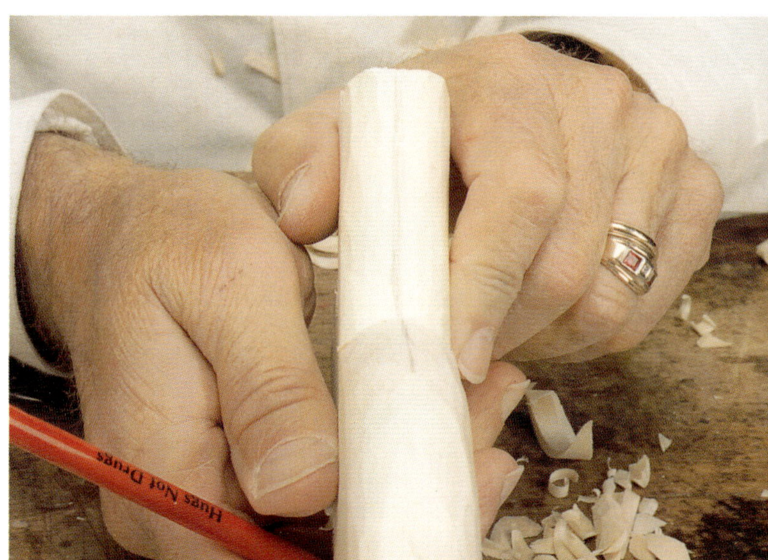

The bottom of the arms are rounded, and the line is still there.

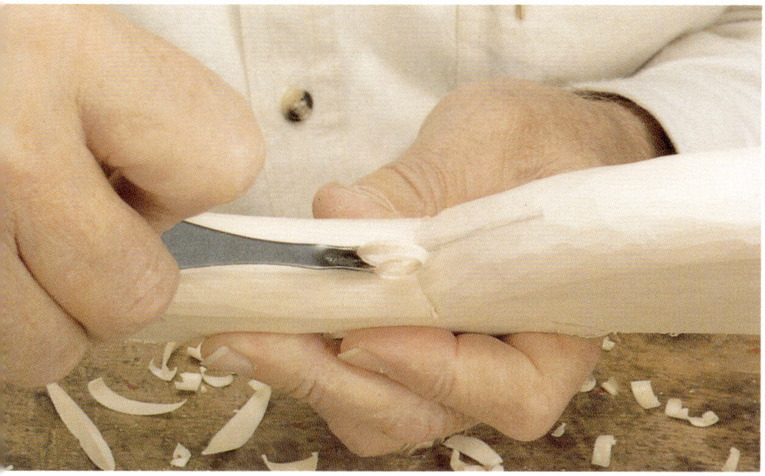

Separate the arms with the gouge tool.

I have drawn in the separation between the arms.

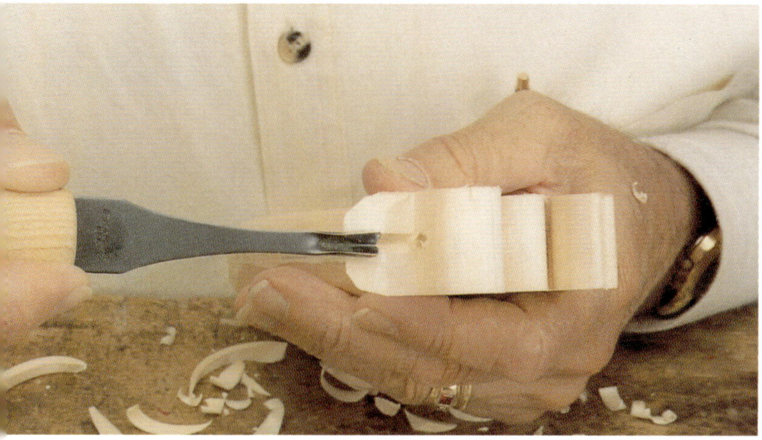

I have also separated the sleeves where they come into the hand with the Flexcut gouge tool.

Cut the separation out with the v-gouge.

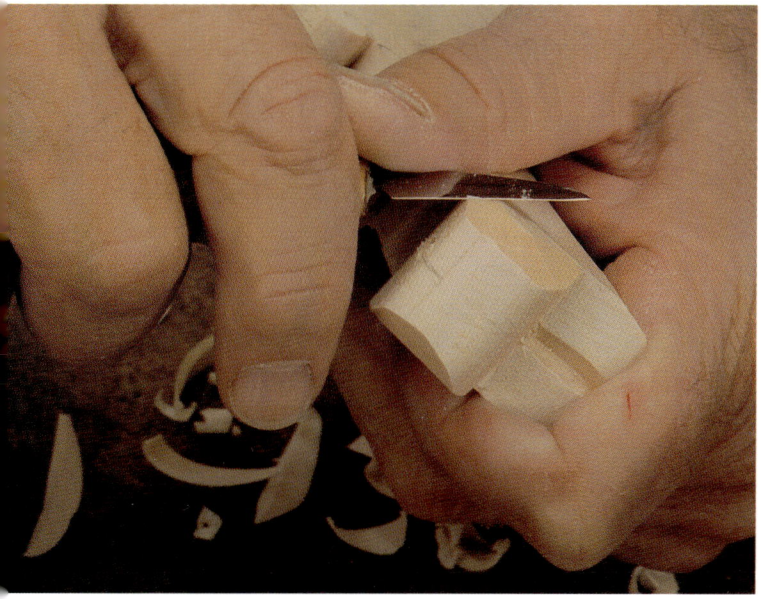

Begin to shape the hands.

Make a v-cut where the top part of the dress meets the hair on either side.

Round each side toward the center line you have drawn in.

Do this on both sides.

Remove the wood from under hair.

Begin to shape the face, chin first.

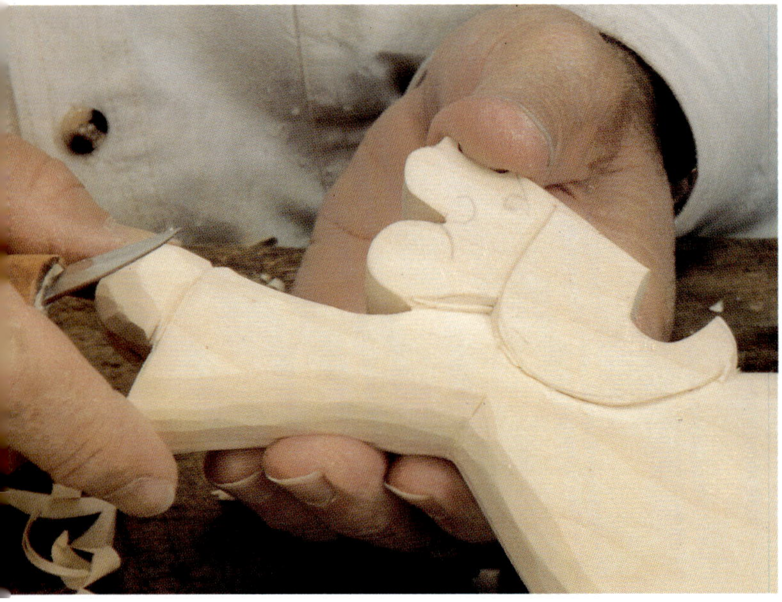

And also under the chin.

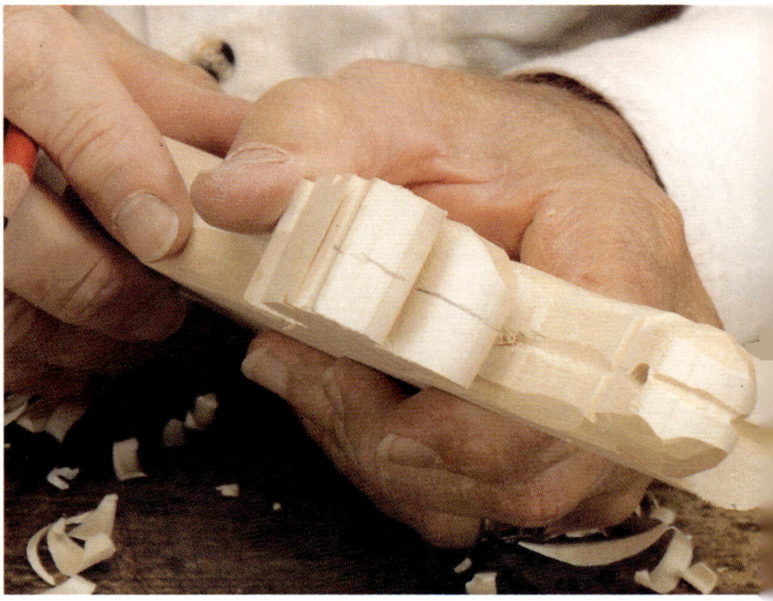

A center line may be helpful, even when doing this face.

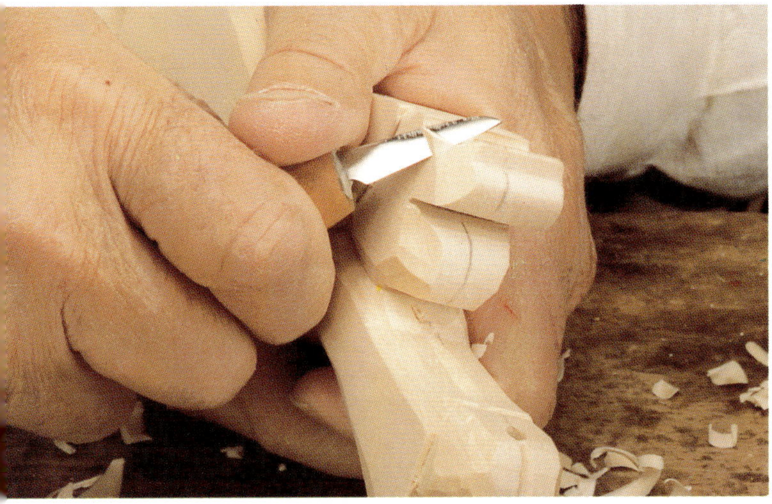

Start to shape the nose.

Cut out a little area where a happy mouth goes, on each side.

Continue to shape nose, being careful not to cut off wart.

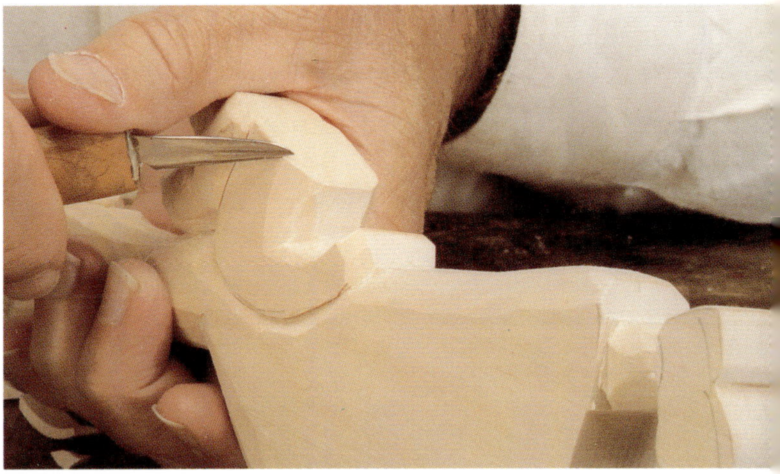

Begin to shape and round hair area.

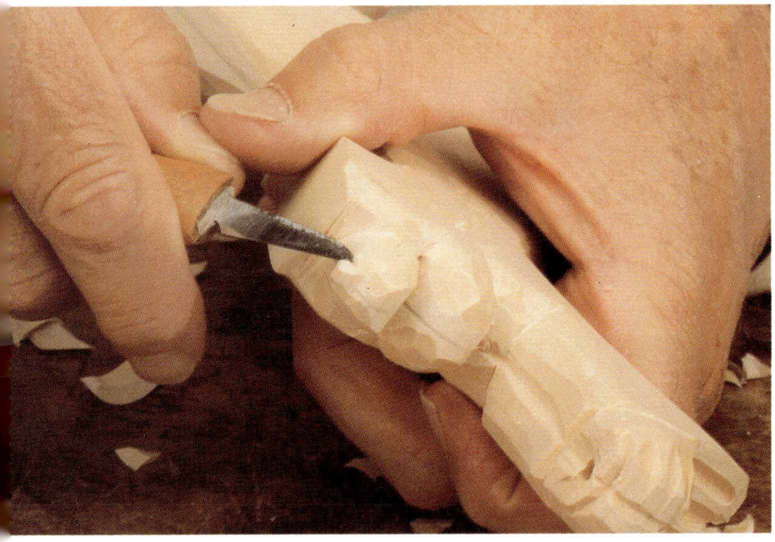

Round the wart, and continue to round the nose to your liking.

I have put in the fingers, using the gouge, on one side.

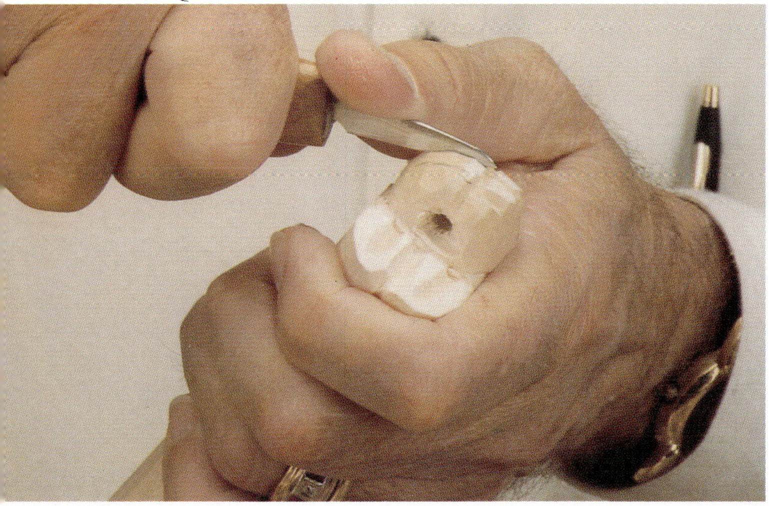

On the other side, I will show you how to do it with a knife. Make a cut down the middle of the hand and cut away from each side.

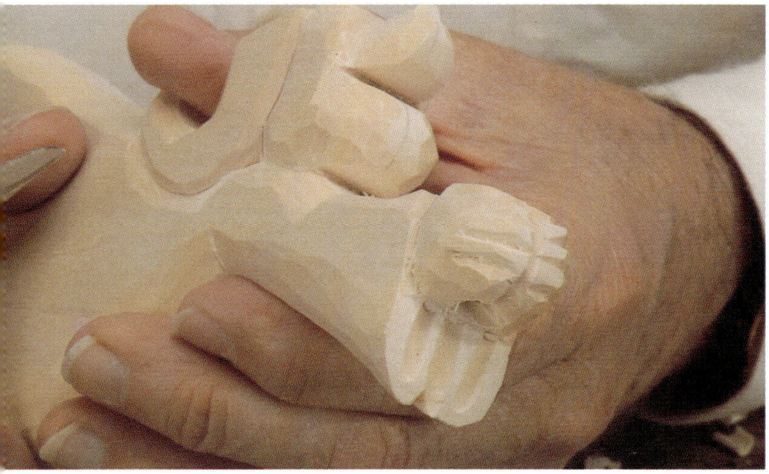

The fingers on this side were done with the knife. This is shown for those of you who do not have gouges to work with.

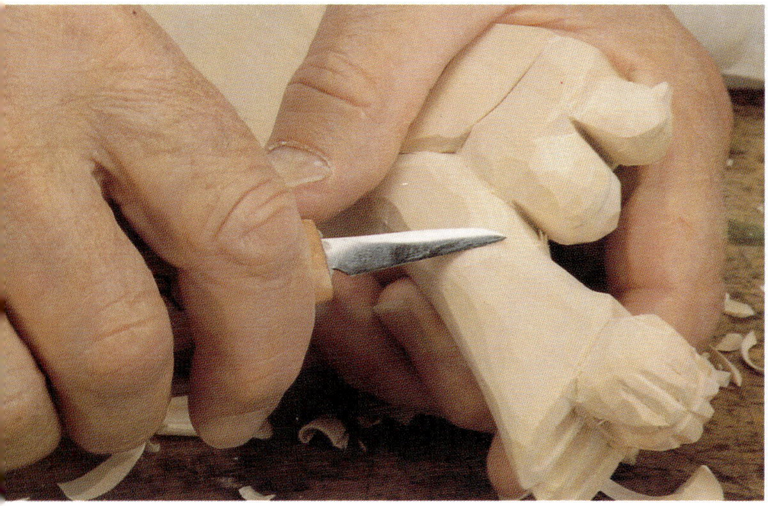

Cut a small notch inside of sleeve to show a little action.

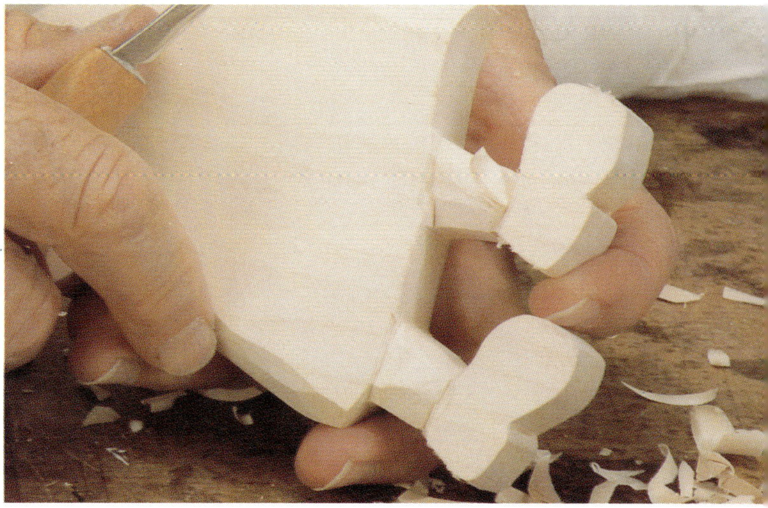

We need to thin out the legs.

The legs are now slimmed.

The shoes will be clunky, but we still want to shape them a little bit.

Add soles with the v-gouge.

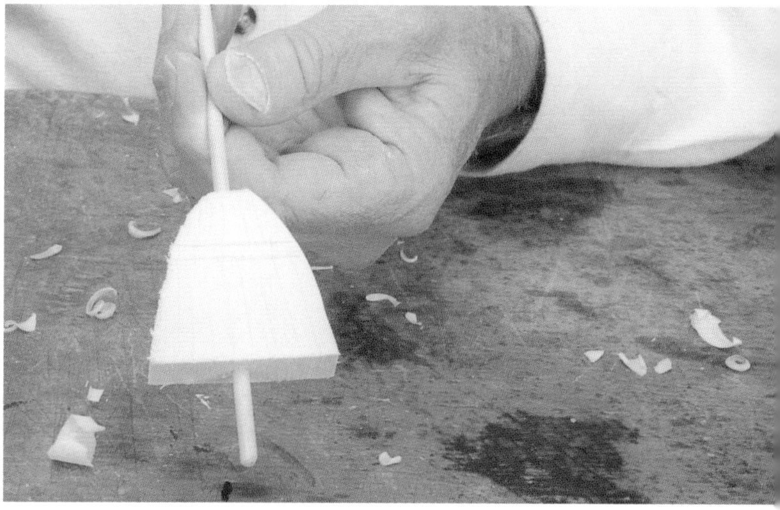

The next piece is the broom. I cut this about 1/2" thick.

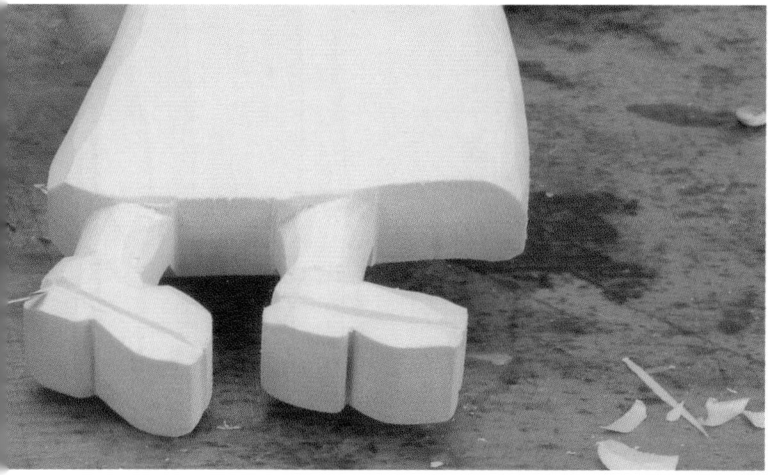

The shaped soles and feet.

Shape the broom.

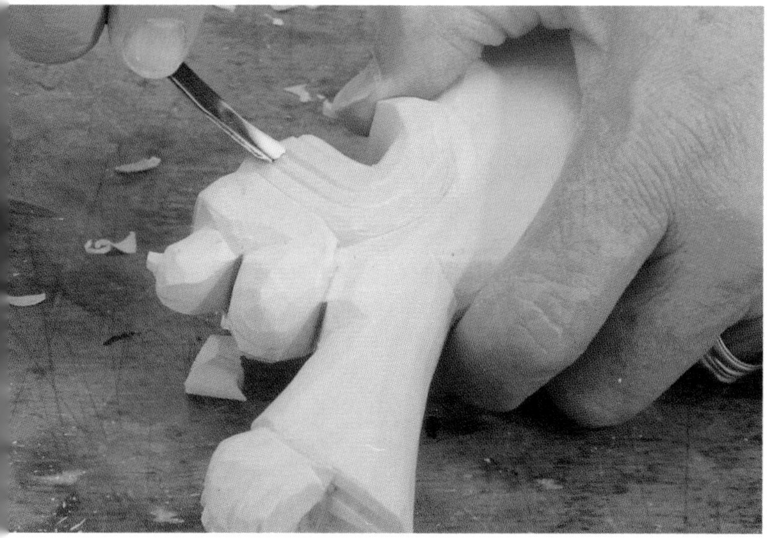

Detail the hair with the v-gouge.

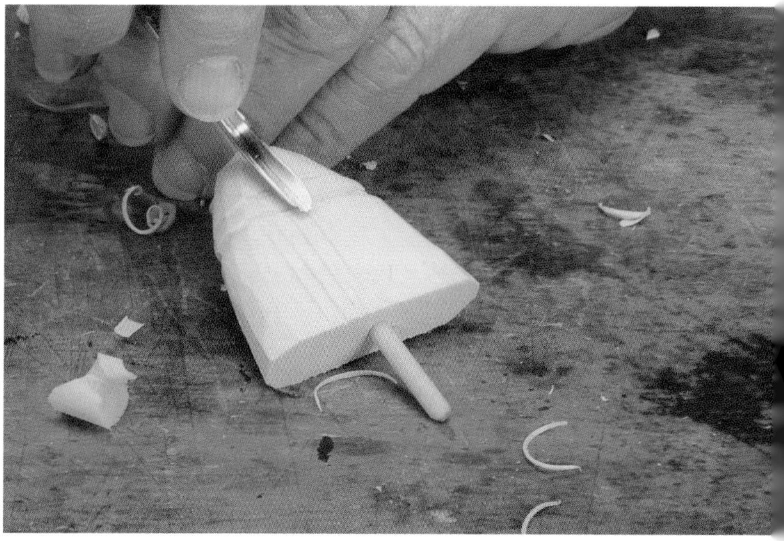

Detail the broom with the gouge.

The finished broom, ready to be painted.

The only thing left is the hat. After it is shaped, epoxy it back onto the head.

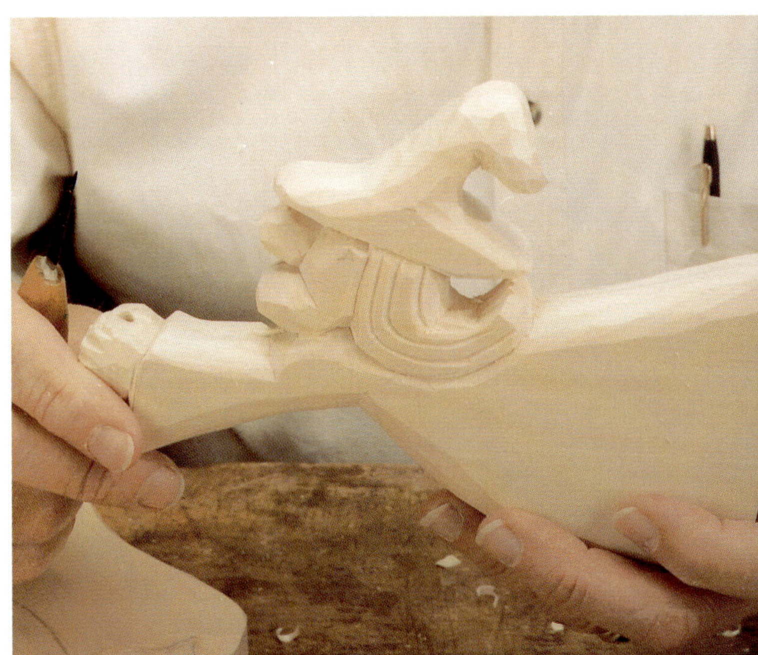

This is my only feat of engineering: bore a hole through the broom, insert dowel (you need a fairly heavy base), and then insert sign "witch parking others will be toad".

I have epoxied the witch's hat on, and she is ready to paint.

Flying Cat

(on its 8th life, at least!)

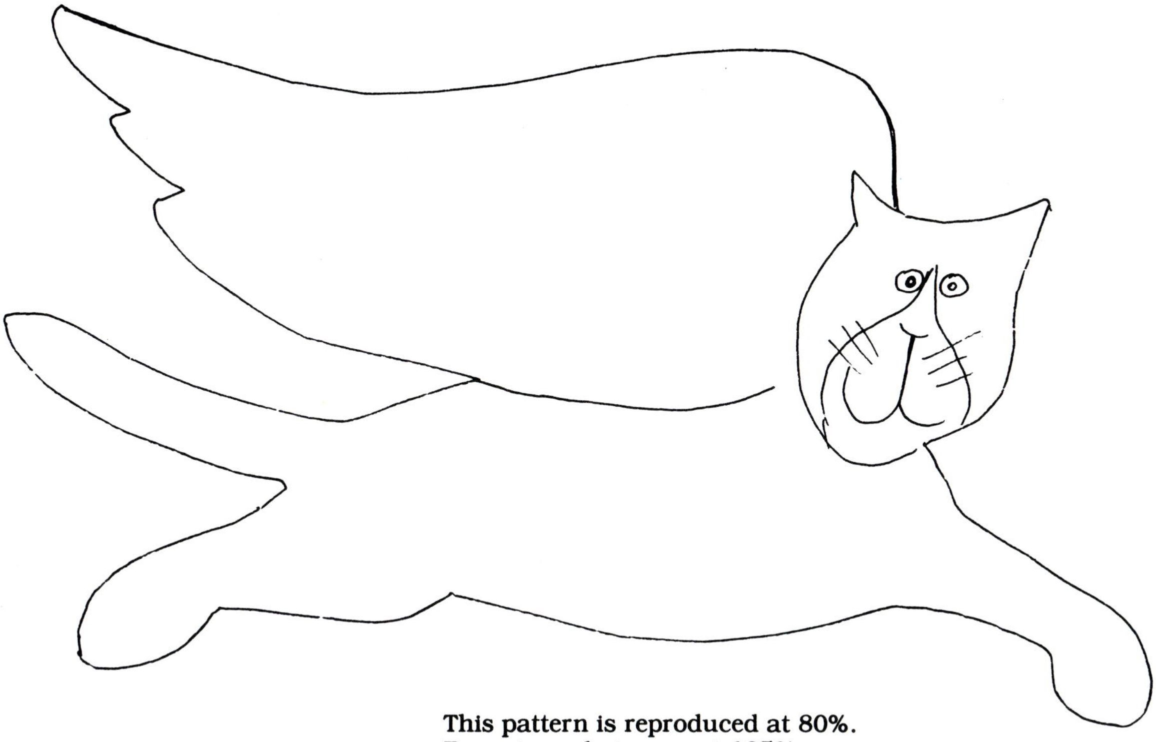

This pattern is reproduced at 80%.
To restore photocopy at 125%.

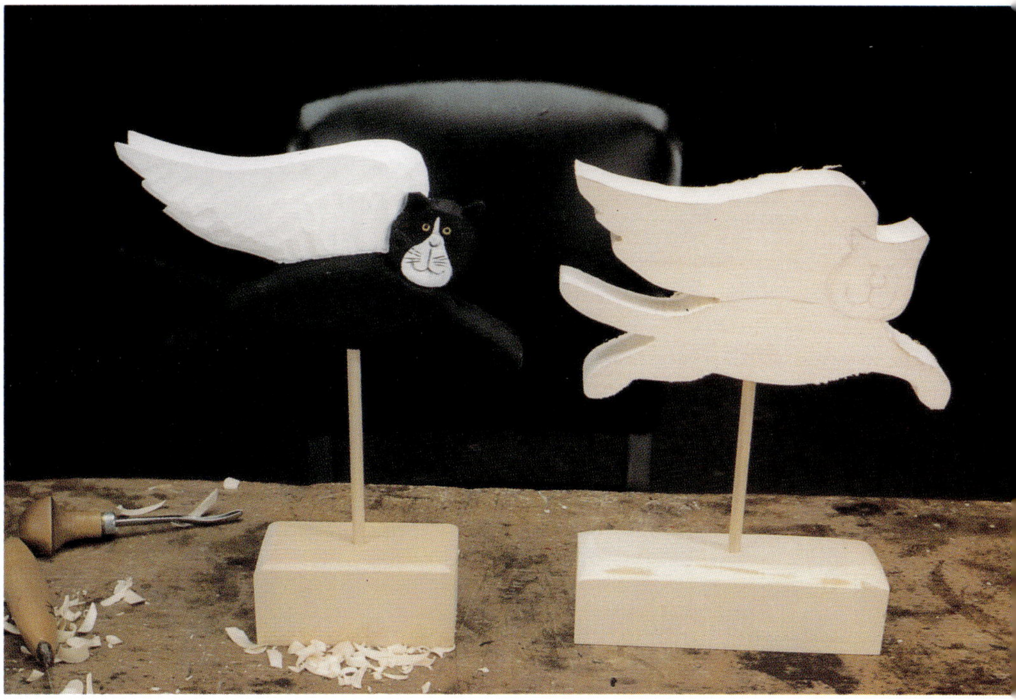

Before and after flying cat.

A center line is helpful in shaping the thin pieces.

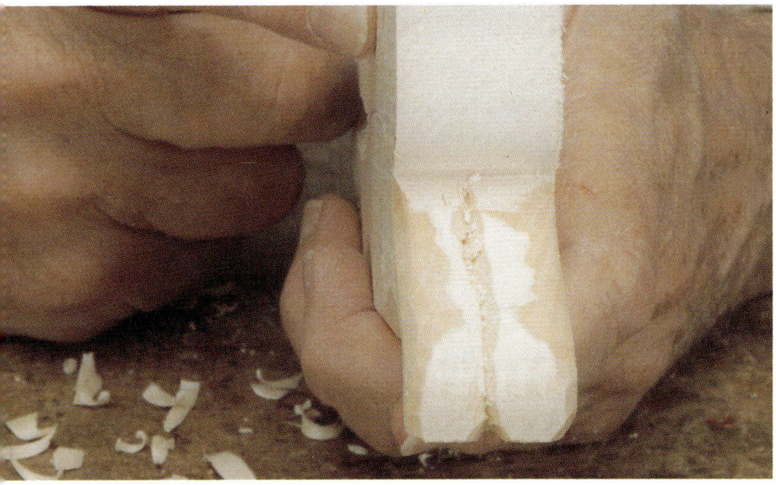

Start by rounding to the center line.

I have rounded a bit, and will now separate the legs. (Not literally, I will just give the impression of the legs being separate.)

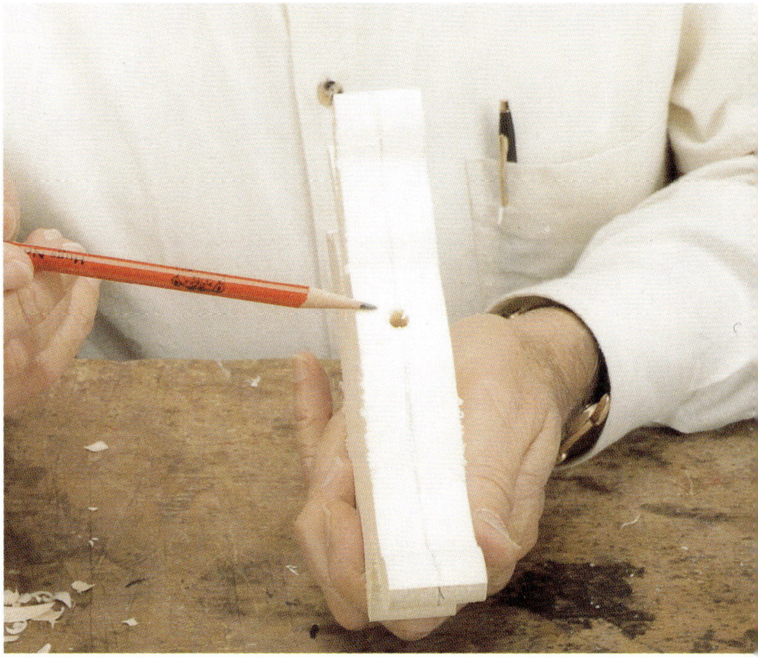

I have done this for the front legs, bottom...

...and top.

Do the same for the hind legs.

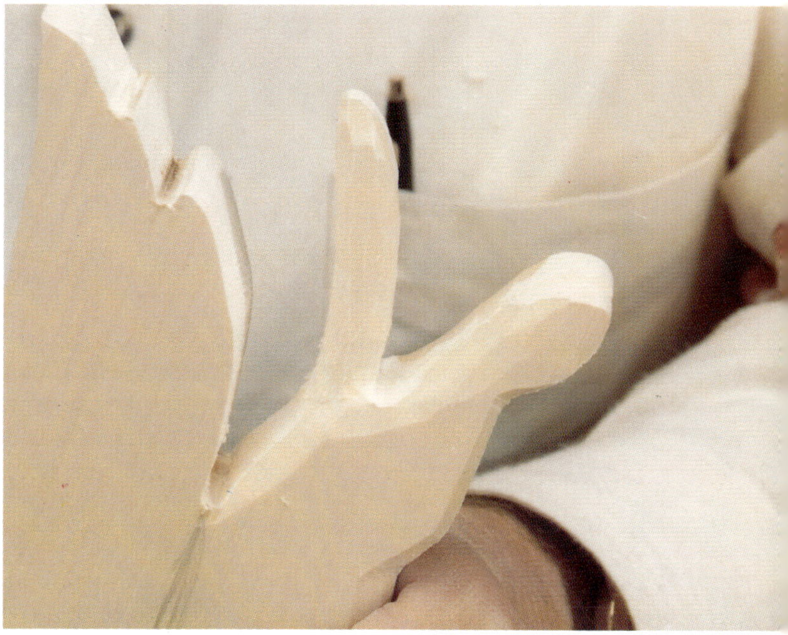

Tail is now getting close to the shape that I like.

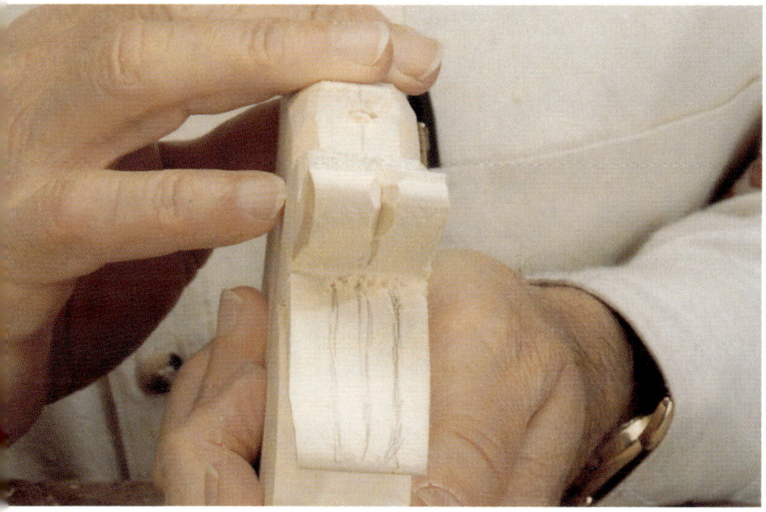

I have drawn another line on the tail, showing how much of it needs to be trimmed down.

Incise around the cat's head.

The Flexcut gouge is helpful in trimming the tail.

And begin to remove the wood from around it.

Incise between the wing and the cat body, and remove that wood.

Continue to round the back of the cat's head, noticing the ear does not show from the back.

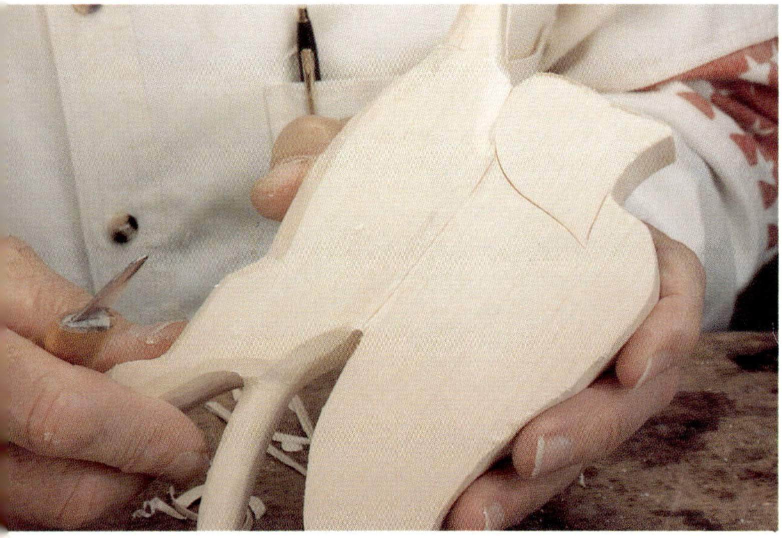

Do the same thing on the back side of the wing and cat head.

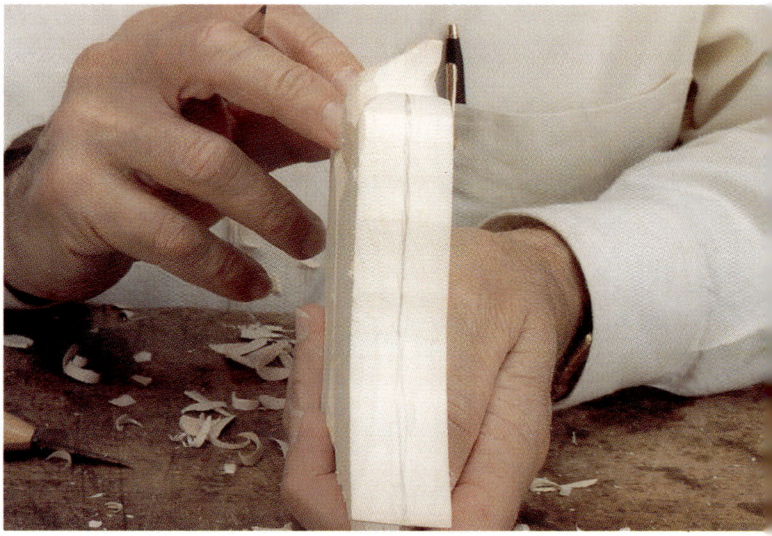

Now we are going to separate the wings.

Begin to round the back of the cat's head.

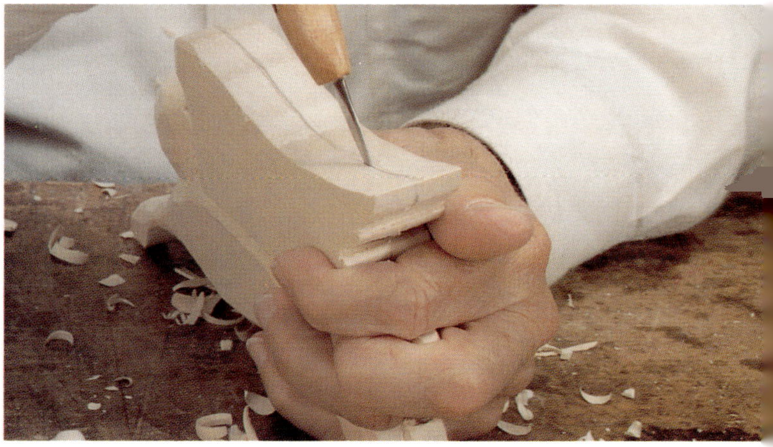

I am doing this by making a nice, deep cut between the wings.

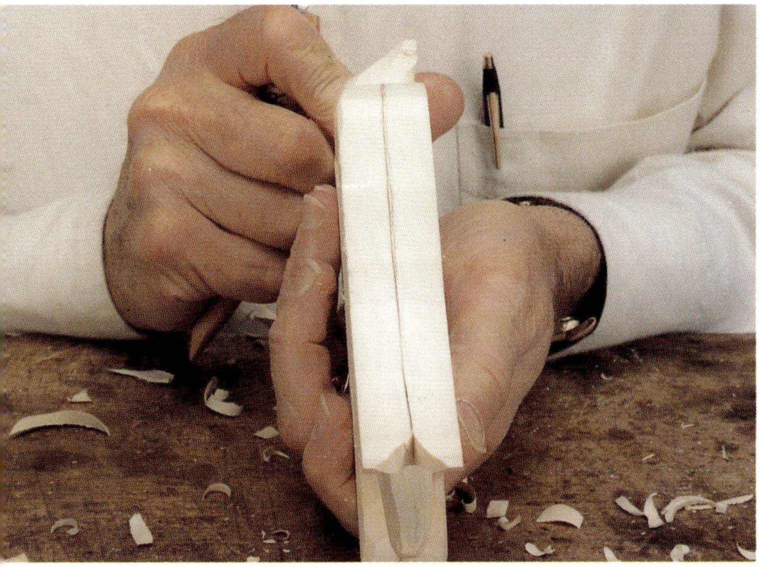

Make a notch in the back.

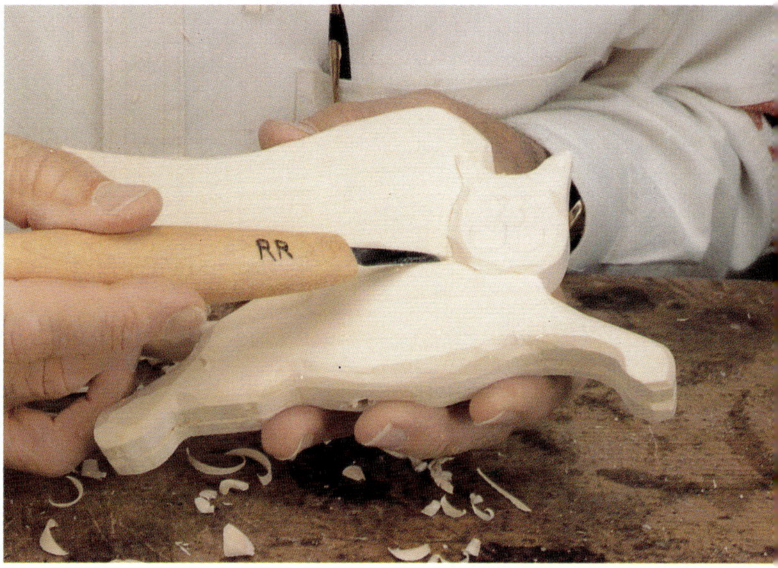

I have continued to round and give the cat's head a little more definition.

I am cutting away the inside with my knife. If you have a large gouge, this would also work.

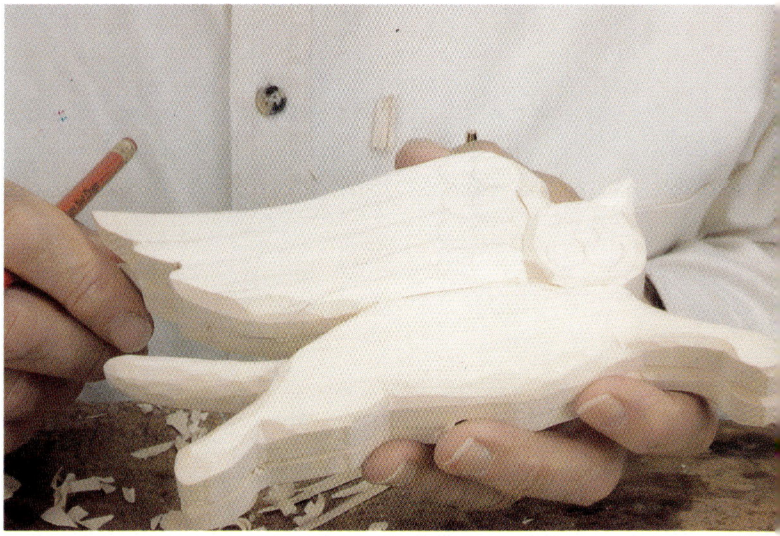

I have drawn in the wings. Here we will be doing them a little differently from the ones on the model you have already seen.

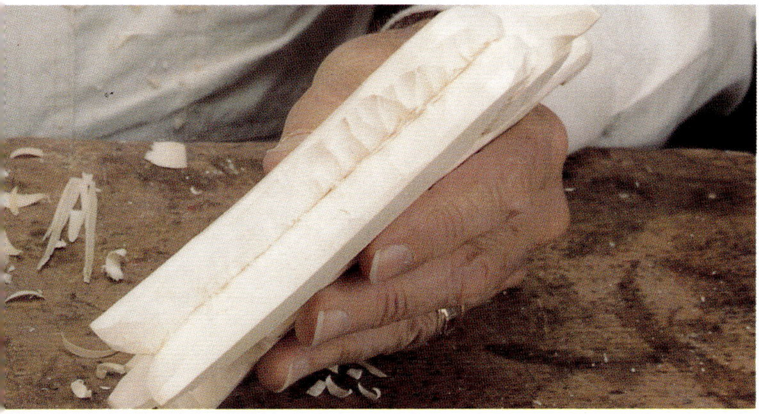

The wings are now pretty well cleaned out.

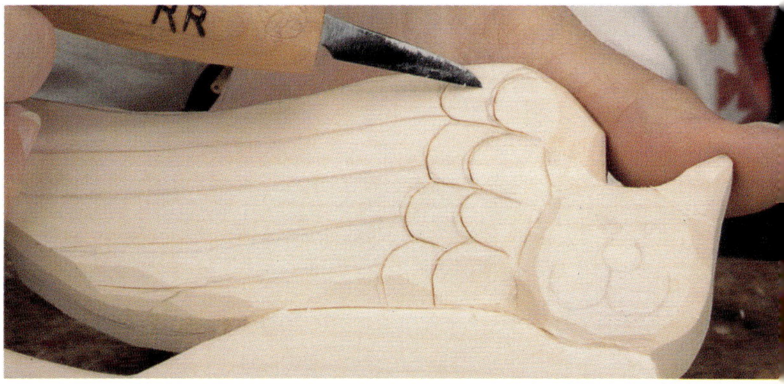

I have incised the feathers of the wing.

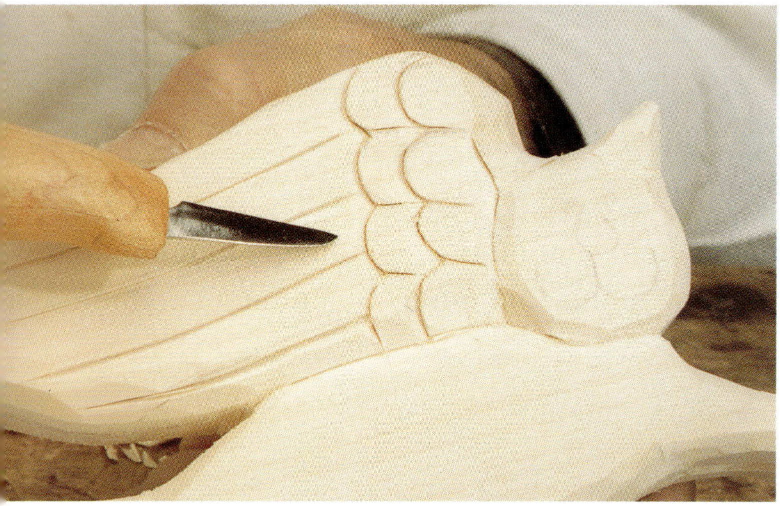

Remove the wood around the areas you have incised.

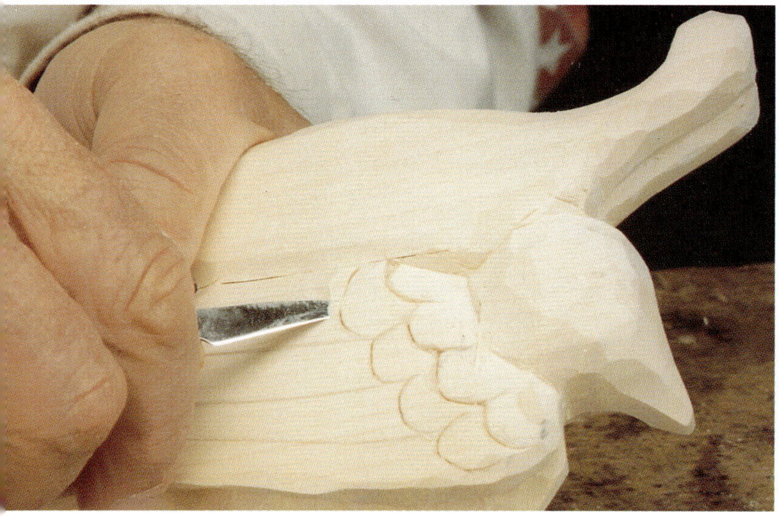

Do the same thing on the other wing.

Use the gouge to take a little nip out of the cat's ears.

I have incised around the cat's nose, and have just taken a little bit out of it as well. Do the same thing for the cheeks.

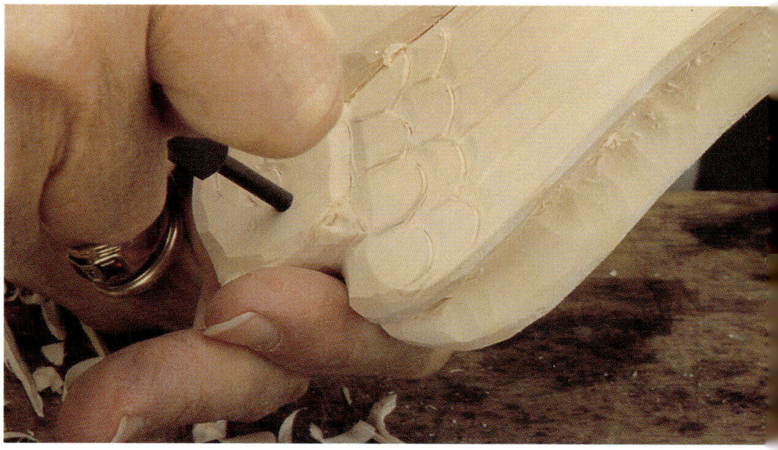

Use the eye punch to make the eyes.

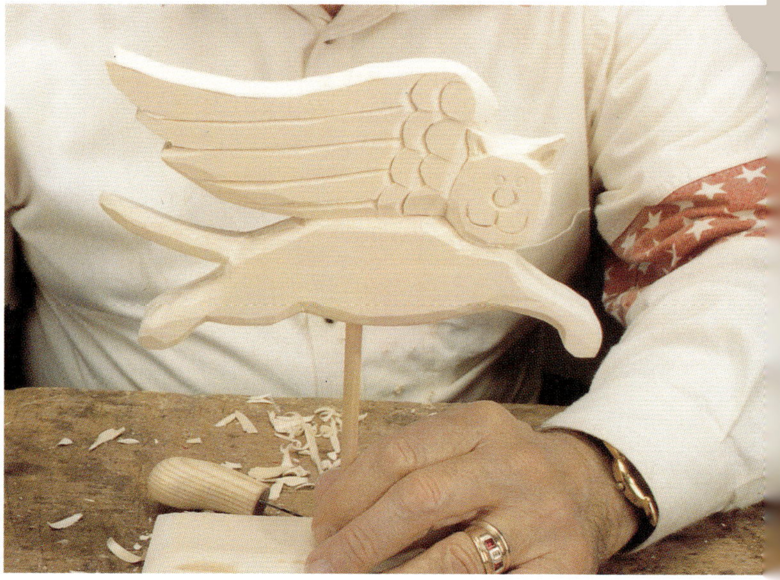

Check the cat for sharp edges and rough spots, and you are now ready to paint!

Headless Jack O'Lantern

This pattern is reproduced at 80%.
To restore photocopy at 125%.

Before and after.

This is a fairly simple figure, the main thing is to round out the body.

We will start by rounding out behind each arm.

Use the gouge to separate left arm from body.

Continuing to round.

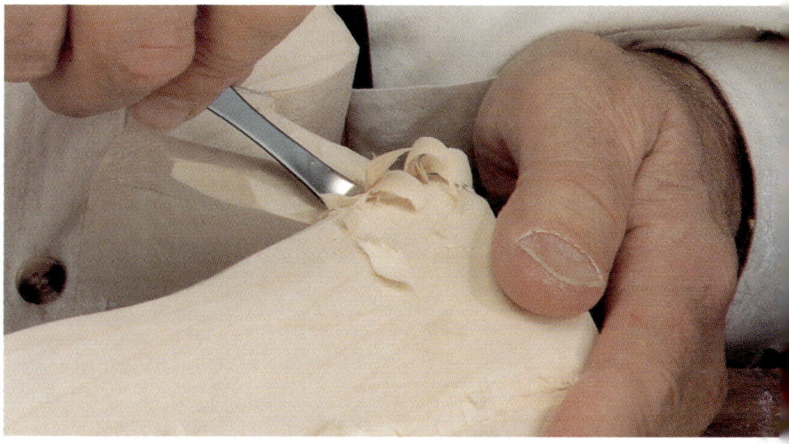

I have found that when carving against the grain, the Flexcut gouge does good work.

I am using the Flexcut gouge to take out around the arms and body.

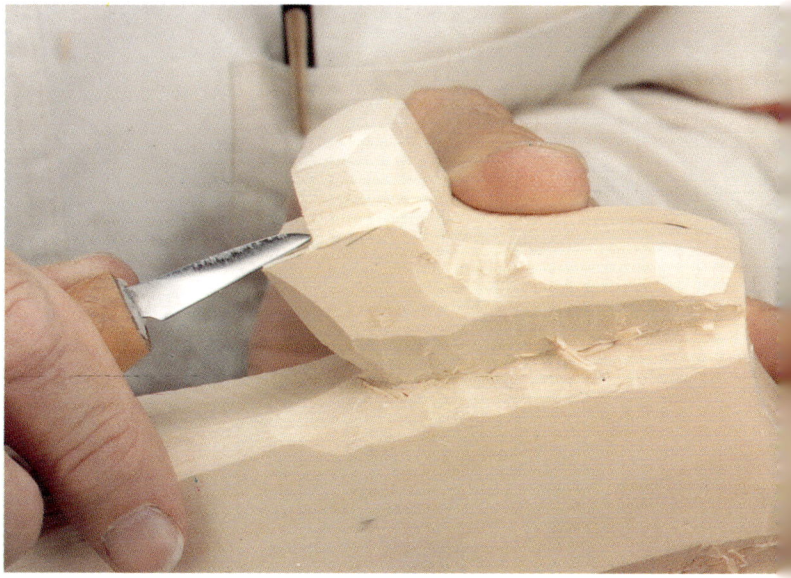

Shaping the hand.

Here I am using the big fishtail gouge because I need to remove a serious amount of wood.

I'm using a Dremel Minimite to remove some of the rough areas that I put in. Continue to shape and round.

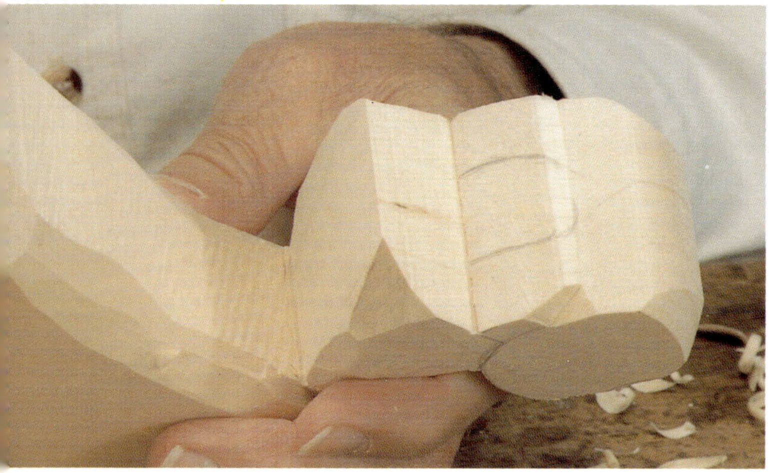

Draw in the hand holding the jack o'lantern before you begin to carve, so you will know how much wood to take away.

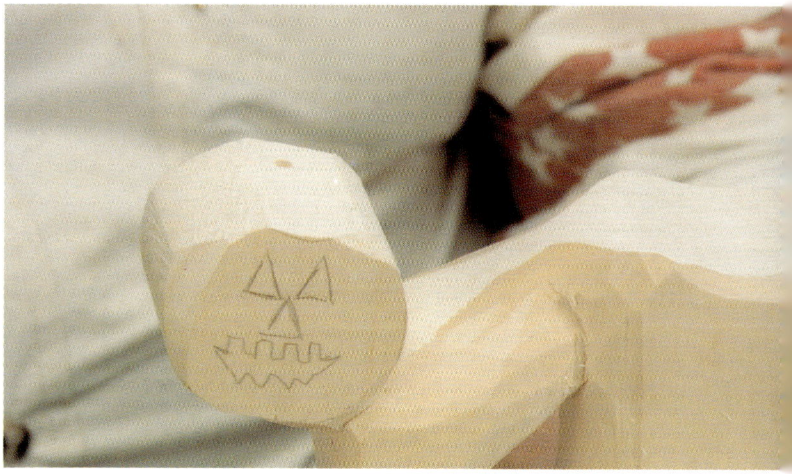

Now we will begin to work on the jack o'lantern. Draw the lines in first.

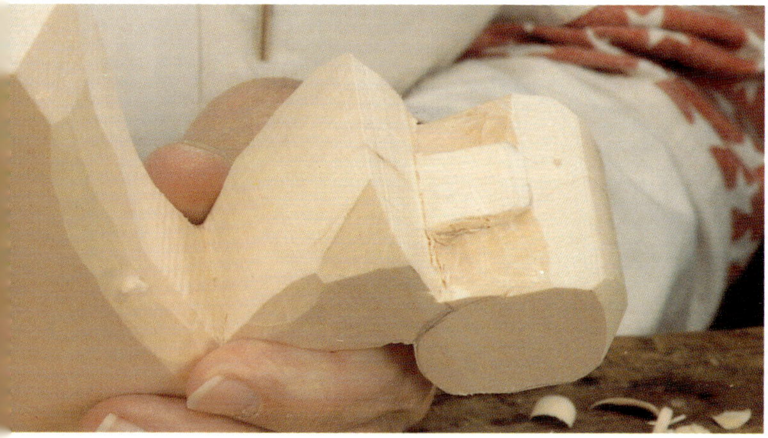

I have now taken the hand down to size. I did it with a knife and a gouge, but you could do it quicker with a power tool if you wanted.

The pumpkin is now beginning to take shape.

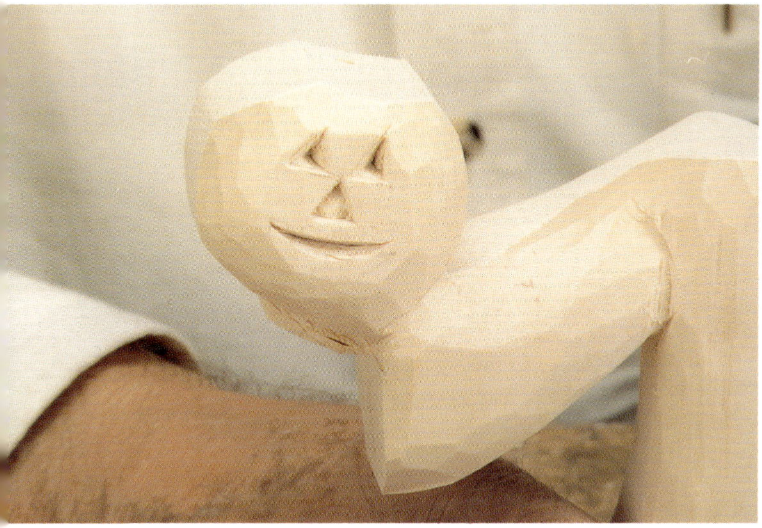

The pumpkin, face finished, before carving in the ridges on the side. Carve the ridges in using a gouge.

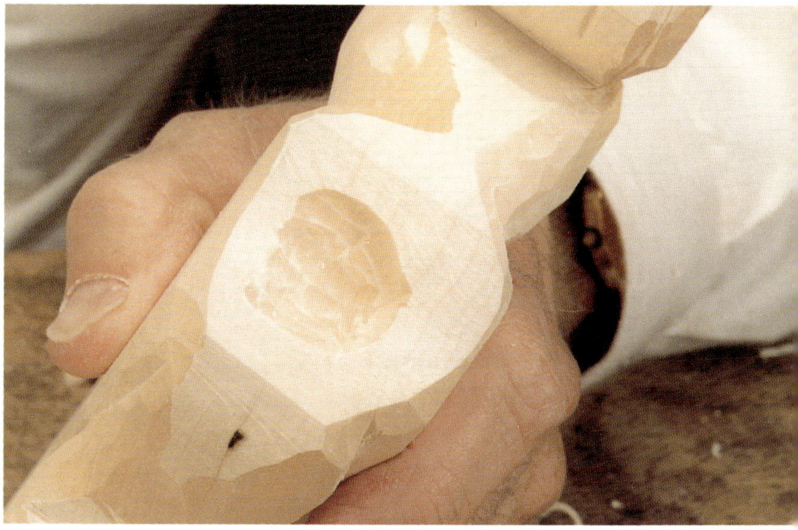

With a gouge, I have taken out the area where the pumpkin head may have come from.

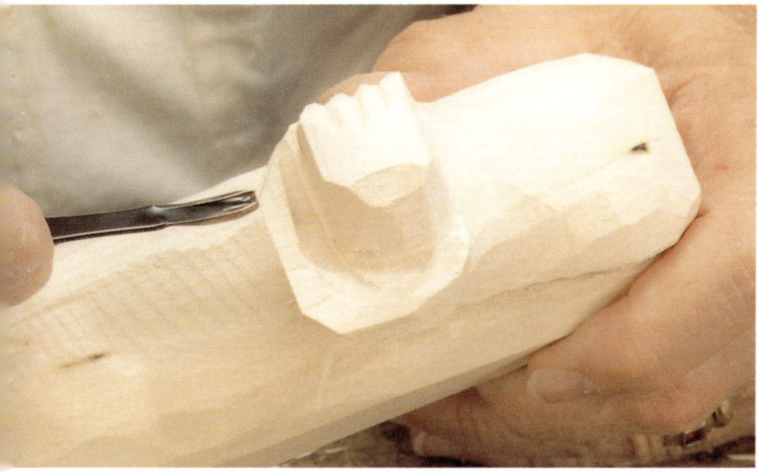

I have drawn in the fingers and am using the gouge to cut them in.

The pattern for the blackbird (and the pitchfork) is with the pattern for this piece.

Using the gouge, take a bit of wood out from under the sleeve.

The finished piece. All I did for the pitchfork was to sharpen the points.

Summertime (Uncle Sam)

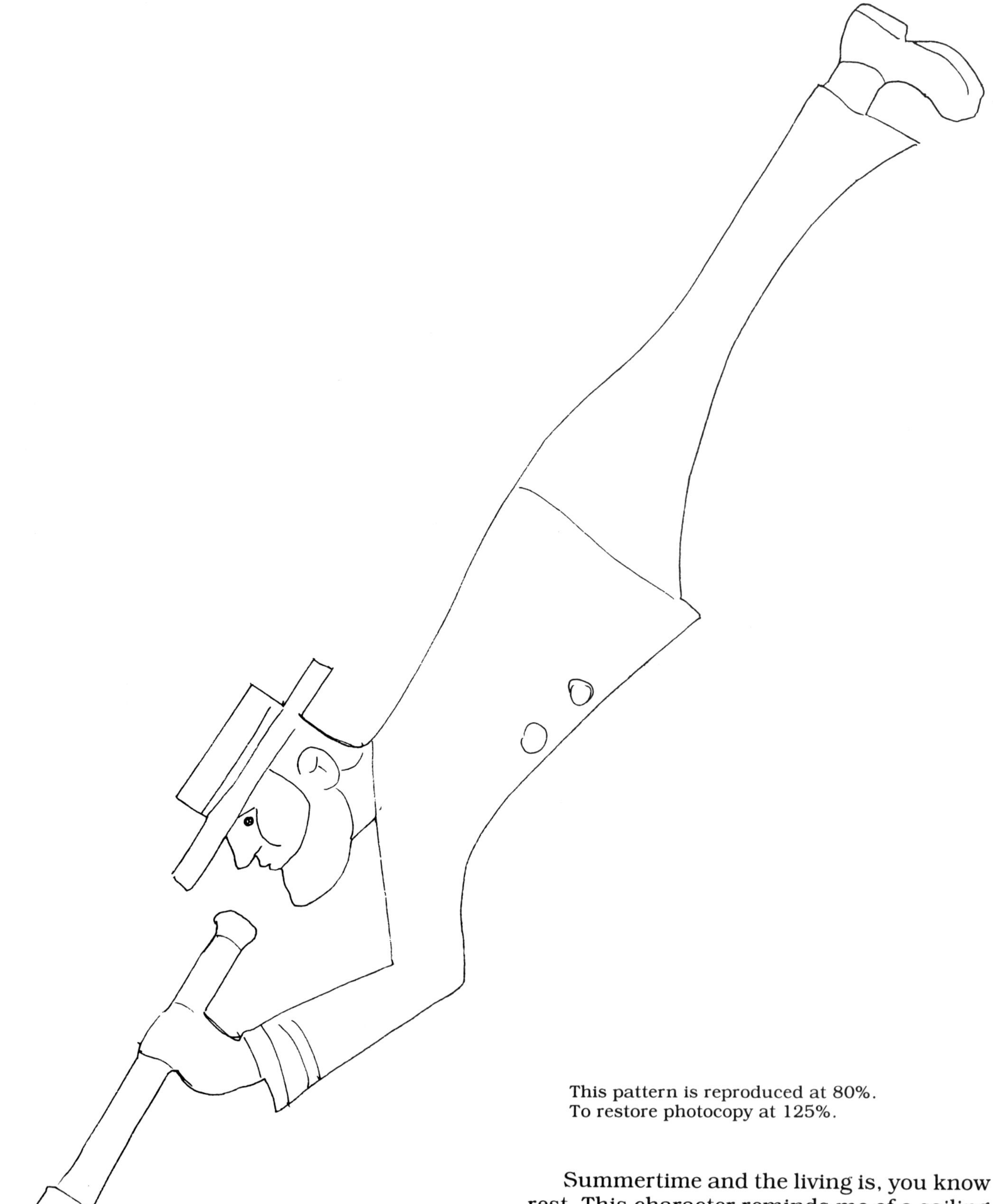

This pattern is reproduced at 80%.
To restore photocopy at 125%.

Summertime and the living is, you know the rest. This character reminds me of a sailing enthusiast. He could also easily be changed to an Uncle Sam and painted for July 4, another celebration day.

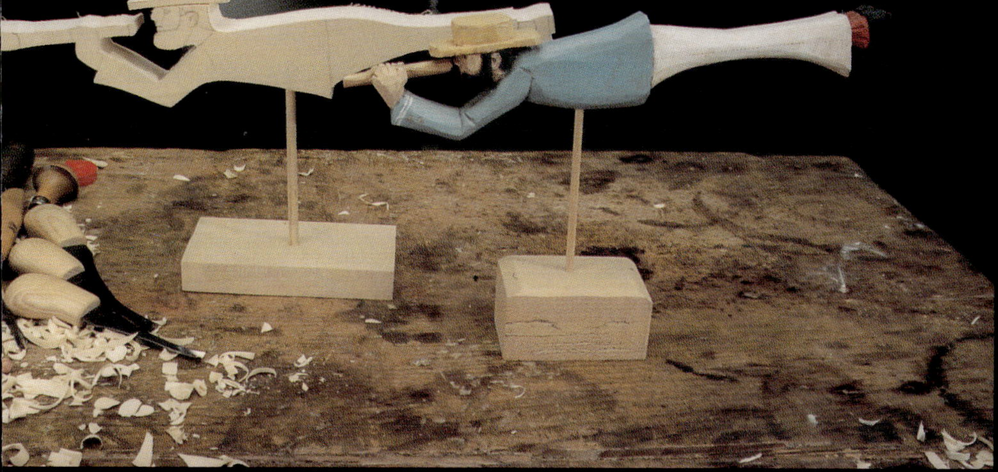

A finished and unfinished Summertime piece.

Start by rounding into the center line.

The arms are separated.

Rounding the top of the arms.

Now carve a line of separation between the legs.

Incise between the arms and between the arms and the hands.

Here I am showing how to separate the legs using a gouge instead of a knife.

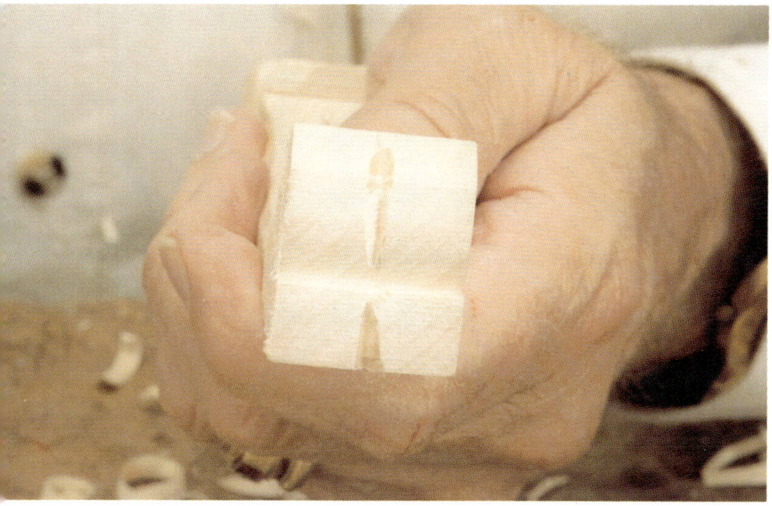

Separate the shoes with a gouge.

Round the back of the coat on both sides.

I have rounded and separated the ankles from the shoes.

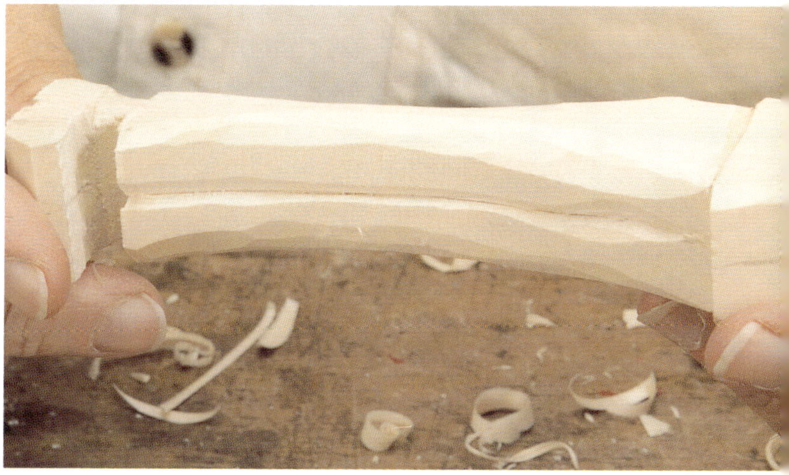

Round the legs on the bottom like so.

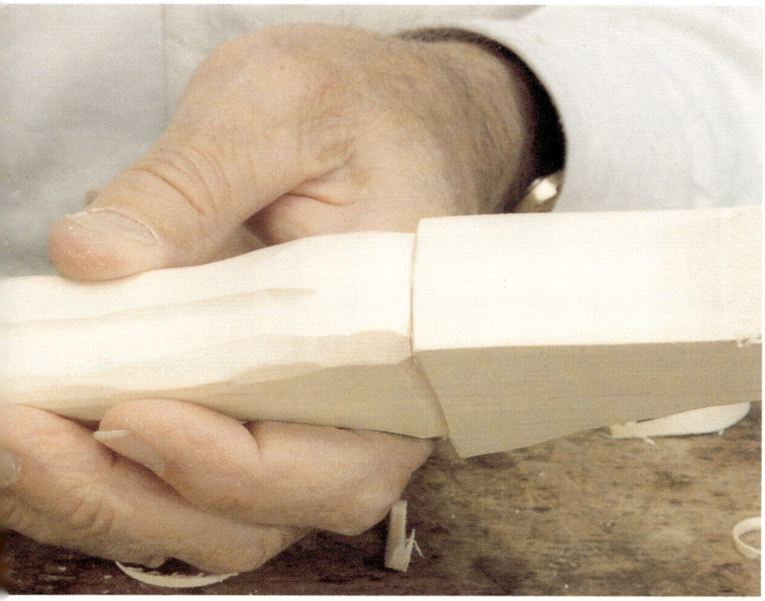

I have separated the trousers from the shirt, and rounded the butt a little.

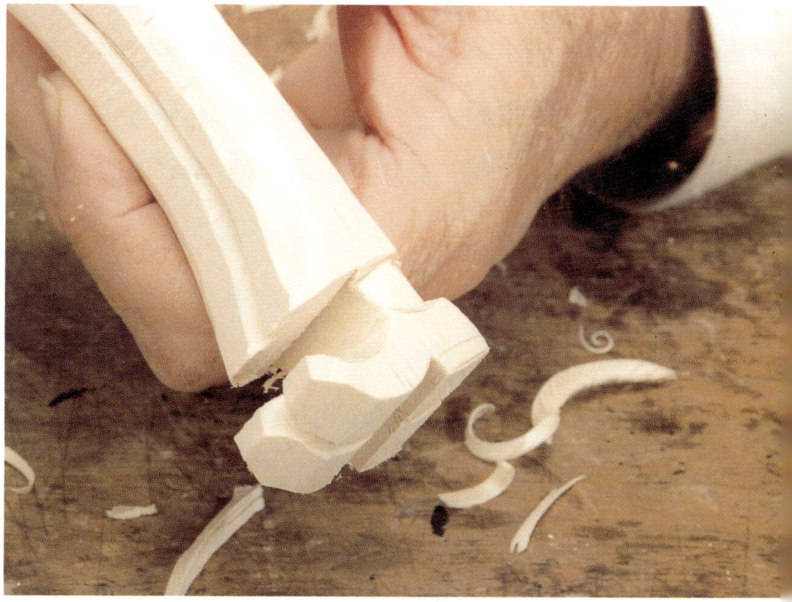

Shape the shoes.

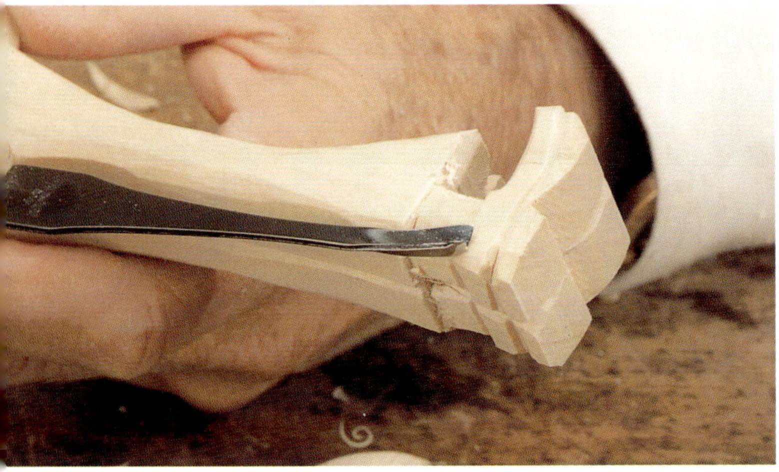

Put the soles on the shoes with the gouge.

I am now beginning to shape the head.

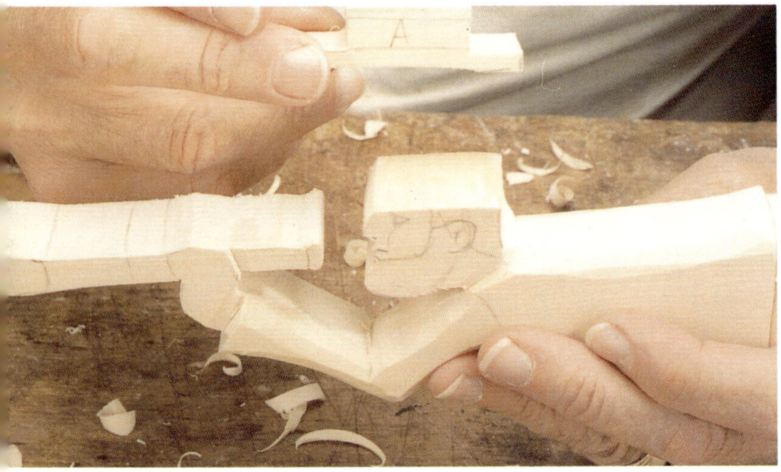

Again you'll notice that I have cut the hat off to detail the face.

To give you a point of reference, it may be a good idea to draw a center line down the face.

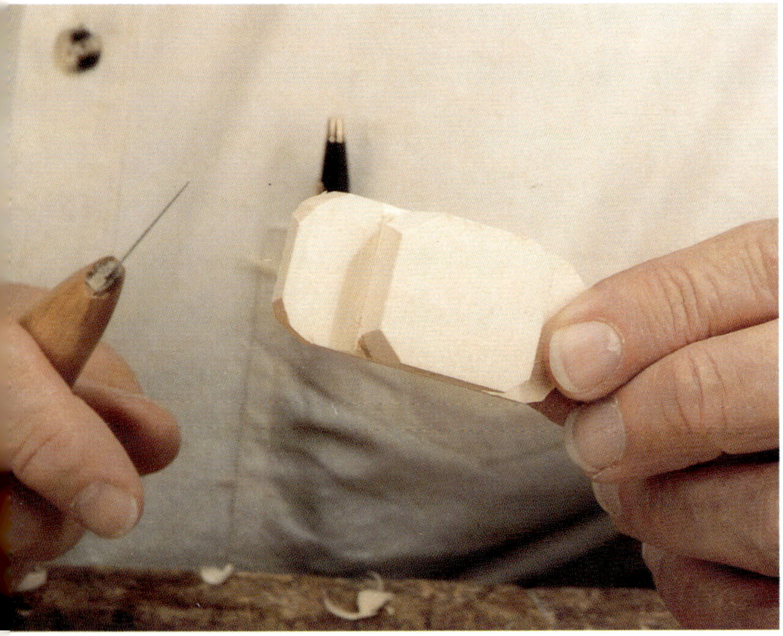

Shaping the straw hat.

Carve away from neck area.

Do this on both sides.

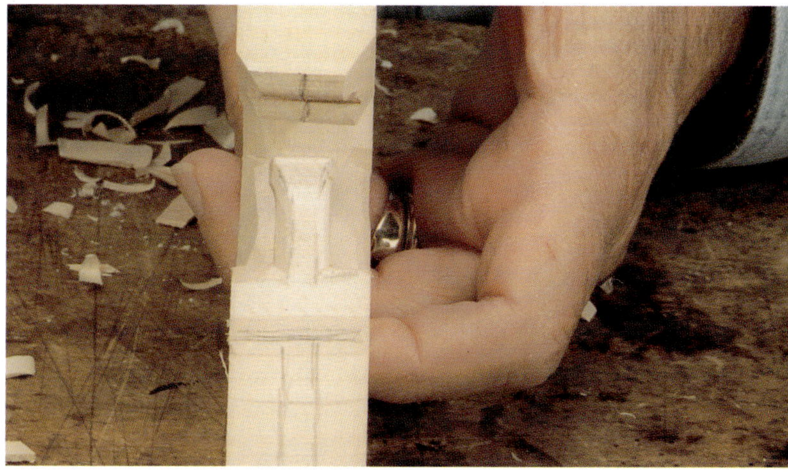

The eyepiece of the telescope.

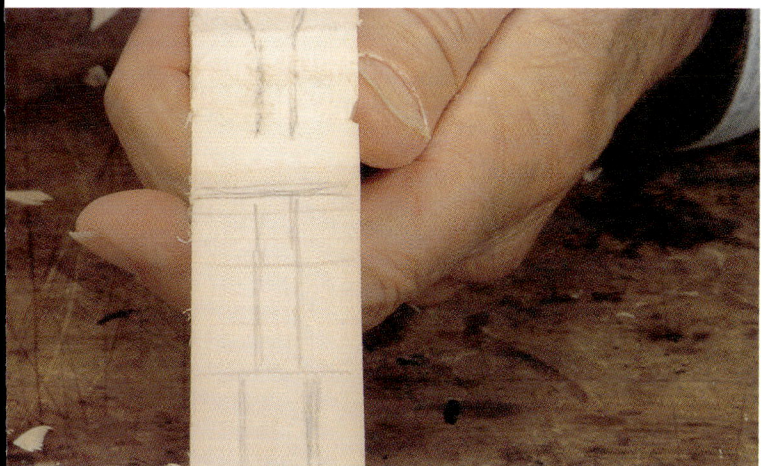

I have found that the thick telescope is getting in the way of my face, so I have started on it next.

A good way of working on this part is to rock the knife back and forth on the lines.

Trim down on all four sides.

Then come back the other direction and take the piece out.

The telescope is almost ready for painting.

I have cut in the left hand with a gouge, just to show you can use either one.

While we are in this area we will go ahead and start shaping the hands.

Do the separation between the arms with a gouge.

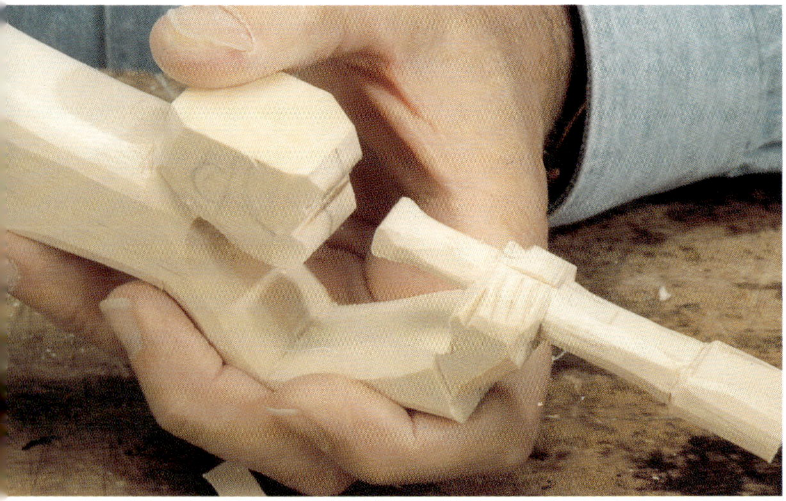

The right hand cut in with a knife.

In the area I couldn't reach with a knife, I used a Dremel Minimite.

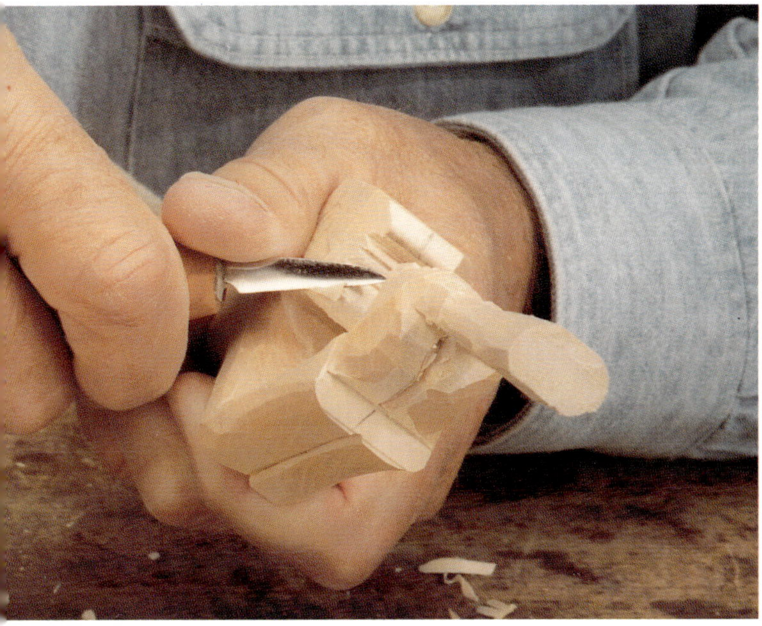

Now that the telescope is out of the way we will begin to work on the face again.

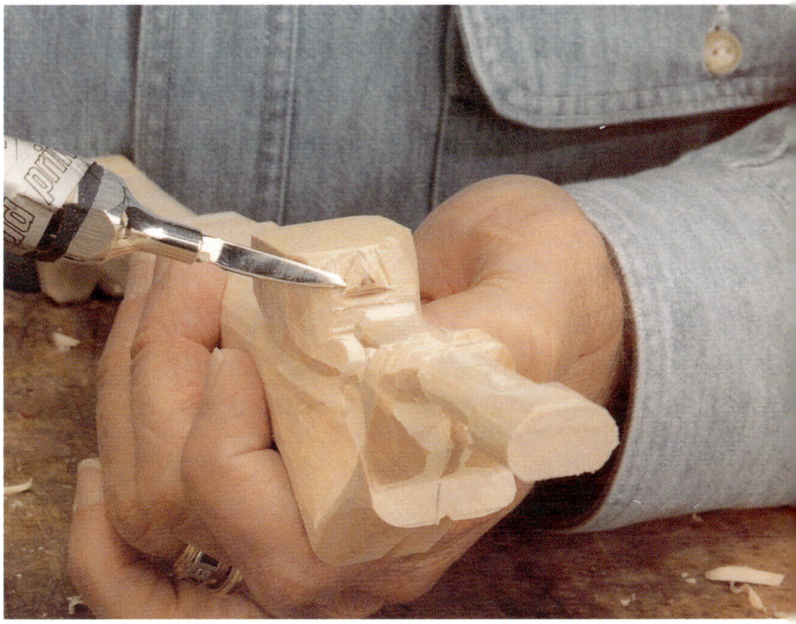

With a small detail knife, clean out around the nose area. And if you want him to look like Pinocchio, you can stick a dowel on the end.

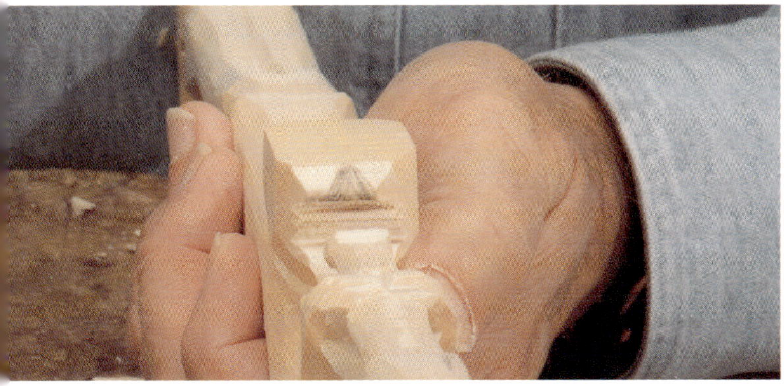

I have darkened the nose area.

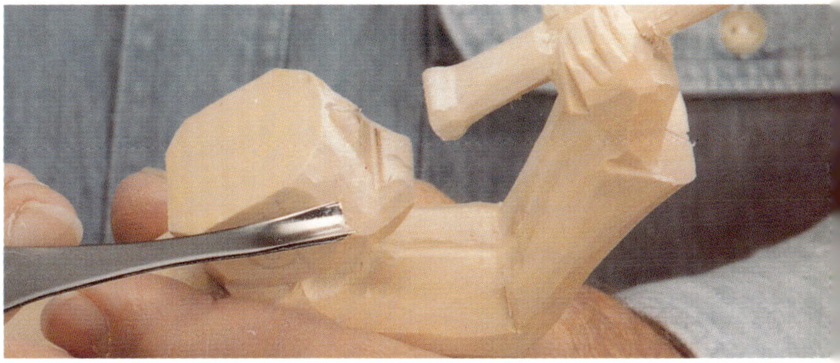

Smooth under the nose with the gouge.

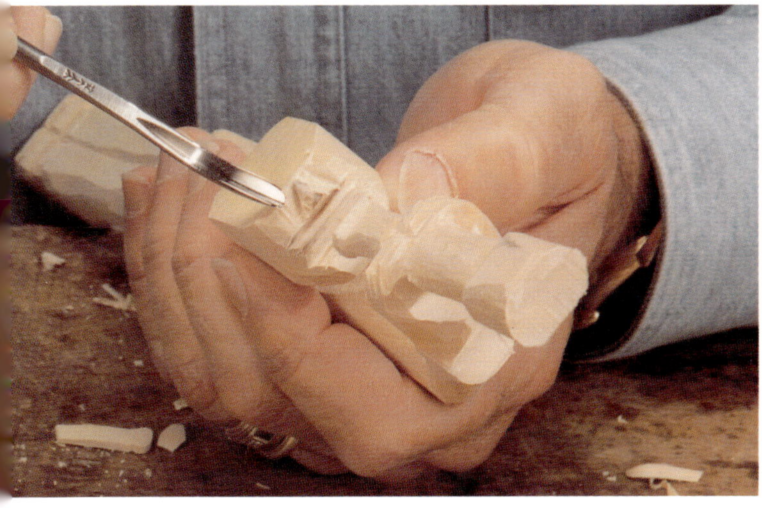

In the nose area, it is very helpful to have a gouge because you are working on the end of the cut.

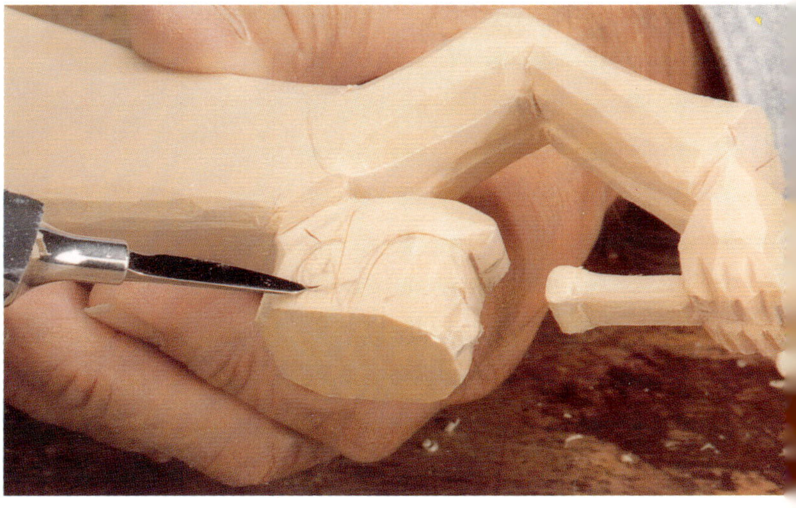

Incise the lines for the ears and beard.

Remove a small amount of wood from the area you have just incised.

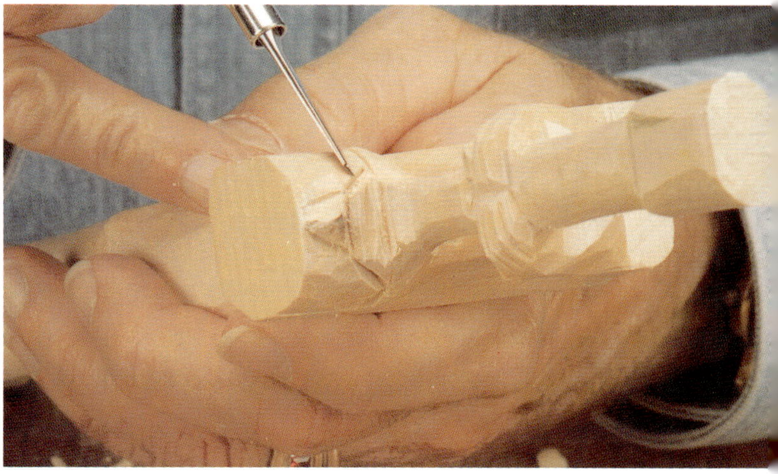

Cut a very small area for the mouth.

Small amount of wood removed from incised lines.

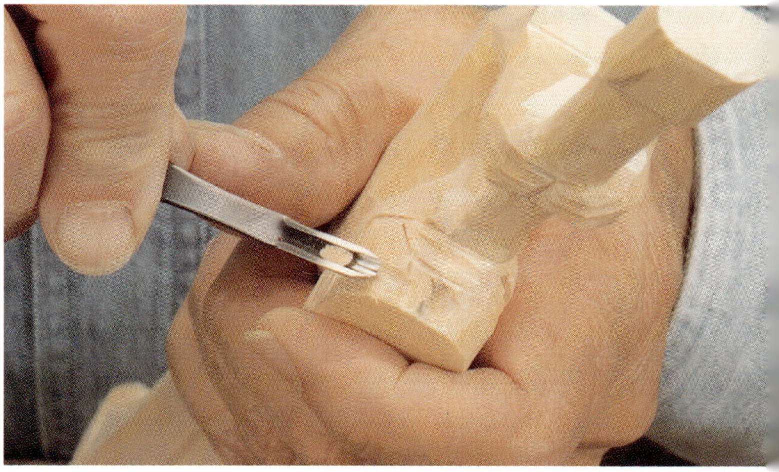

On his left eye, I have made an indentation for his eye to be painted in.

Incise a character line on either side of his nose.

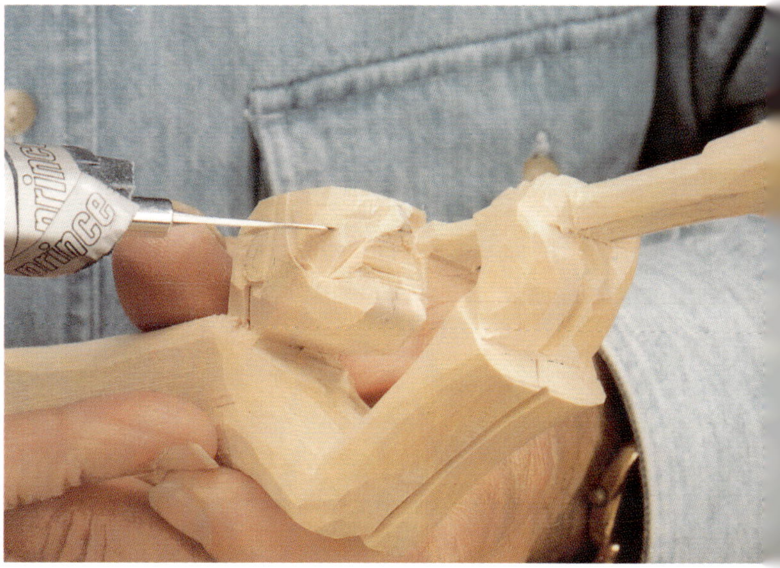

On the right eye, I have just made a small line as the eye will be squinting.

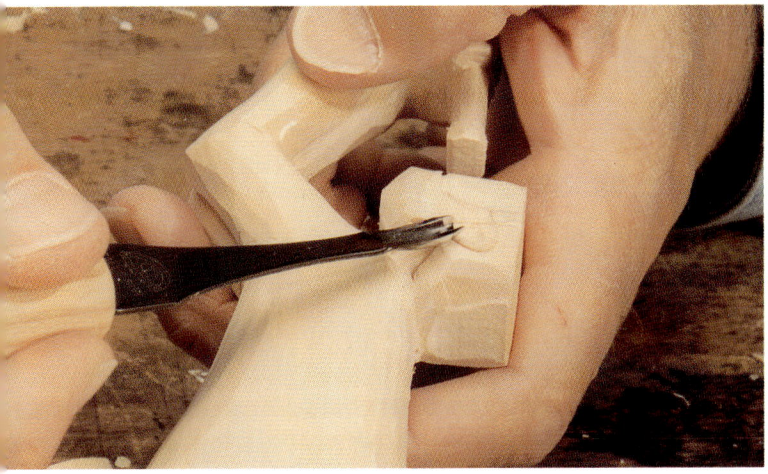

With a gouge, take a small chunk out of the ear to give it a more realistic look.

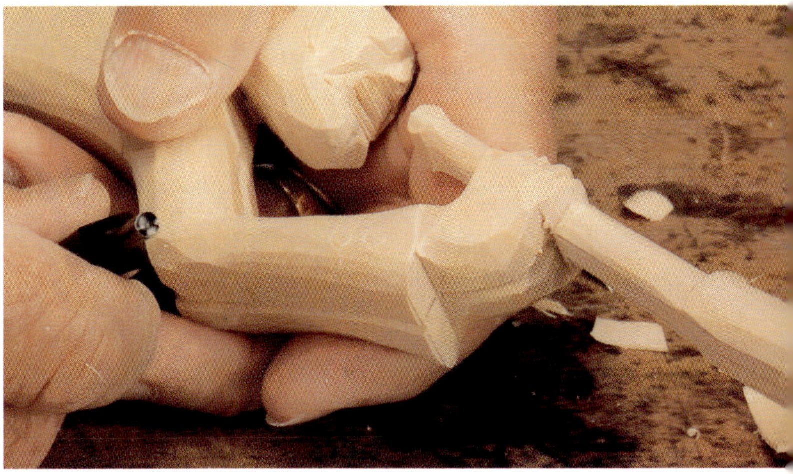

Add buttons on the sleeves with the trusty eye punch.

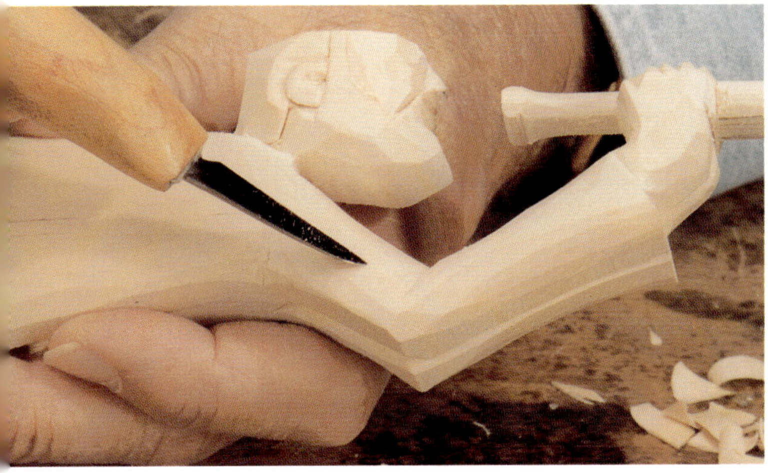

Check your piece over, and check out for small details like the folds in his shirt.

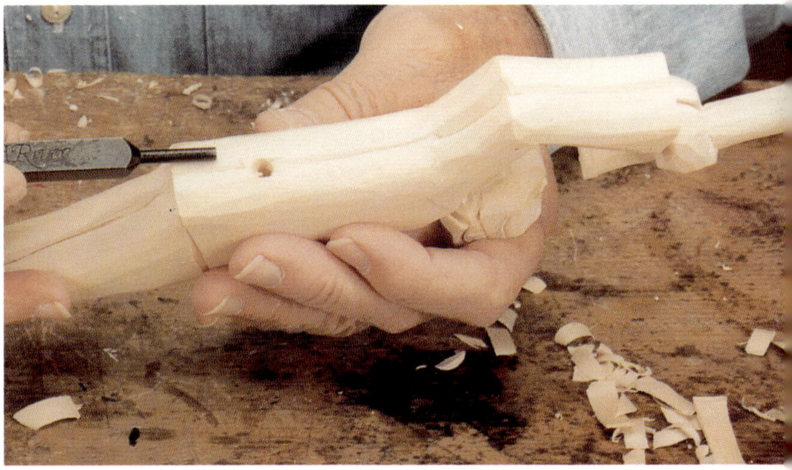

Not that anyone will ever notice, but I have given him buttons on his shirt, also using the eye punch.

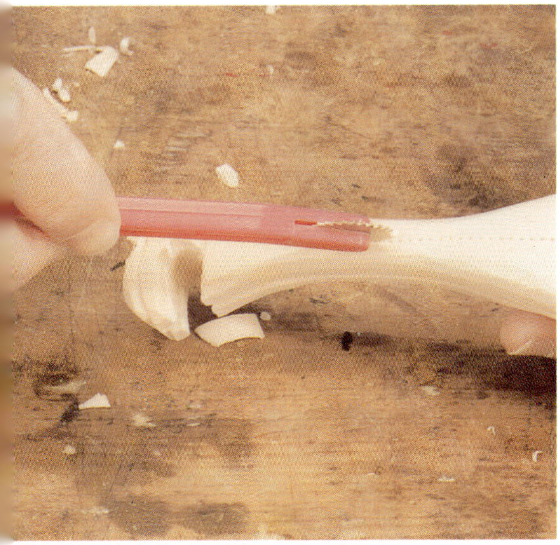

Add stitches on pant legs with a tracing wheel. I got this idea from one of Tom Wolfe's books.

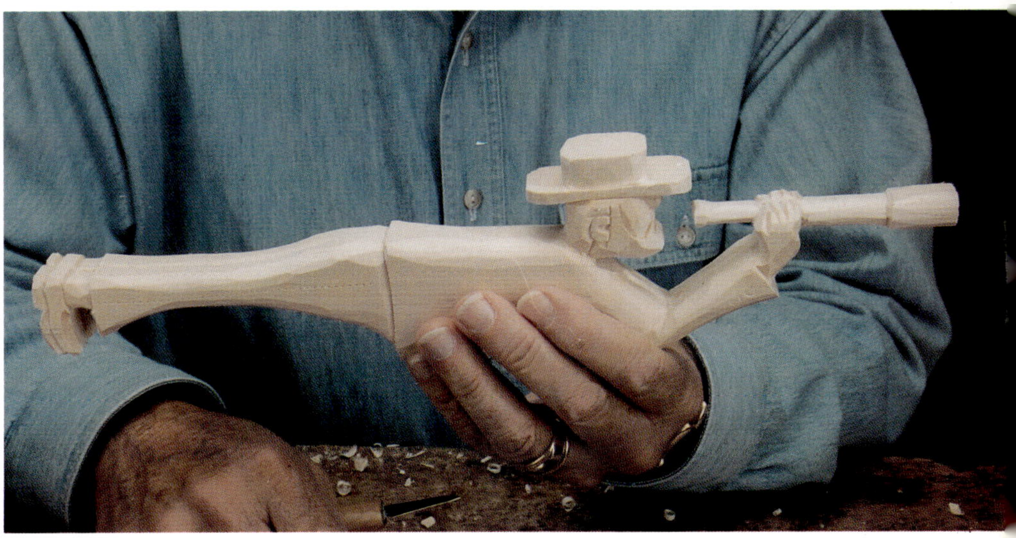

He is ready to paint, in whichever style you choose—the sailor or Uncle Sam.

Painting

These are the paints we will be using.

The Flying Witch

Start with black because it is the prominent color.

While you have the black paint out, be sure to paint the wart and the shoes as well.

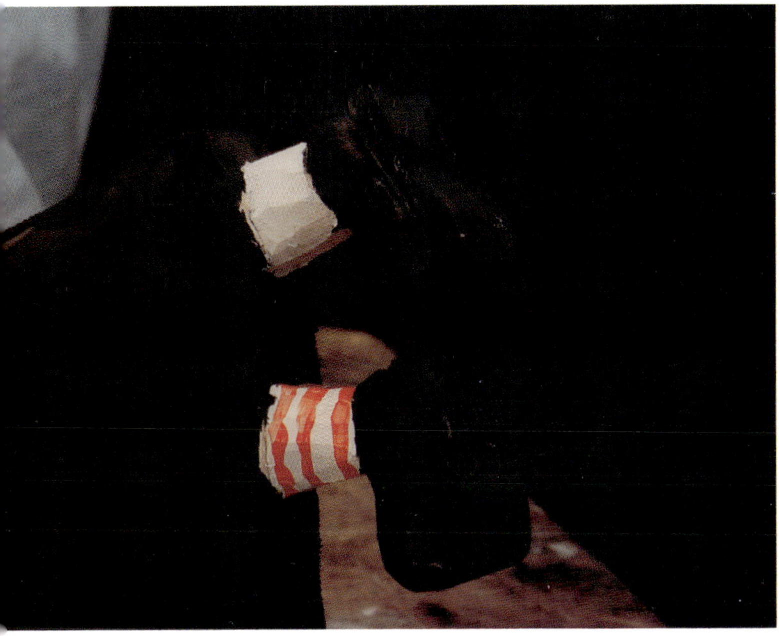

Paint the stockings white and add orange stripes, after allowing white paint to dry.

Paint the broom yellow and the base green.

We painted the face and hands flesh colors, two black dots for the eyeballs, and a red slash for the lips. She has a horrible underbite. Before you glue the hat on, you may want to put a hair on the wart, using a thin gauge wire—the coup de grace for this witch.

Add the sign, and either burn or paint in whatever slogan you want.

Paint the clothes and hat Hunter Green.

Light green for the sleeves and lapels.

Beard and eyebrows are orange.

Gold buckles for shoes and hat, and the shoes and hat are black.

Use the same black as we did for the witch.

Robe is grey.

Head is Santa Flesh with a little red and flesh for the cheeks.

Beard is white.

Scythe is silver.

Body is black.

Face is white with black whiskers.

Wings are white.

Yellow eyes with black highlights.

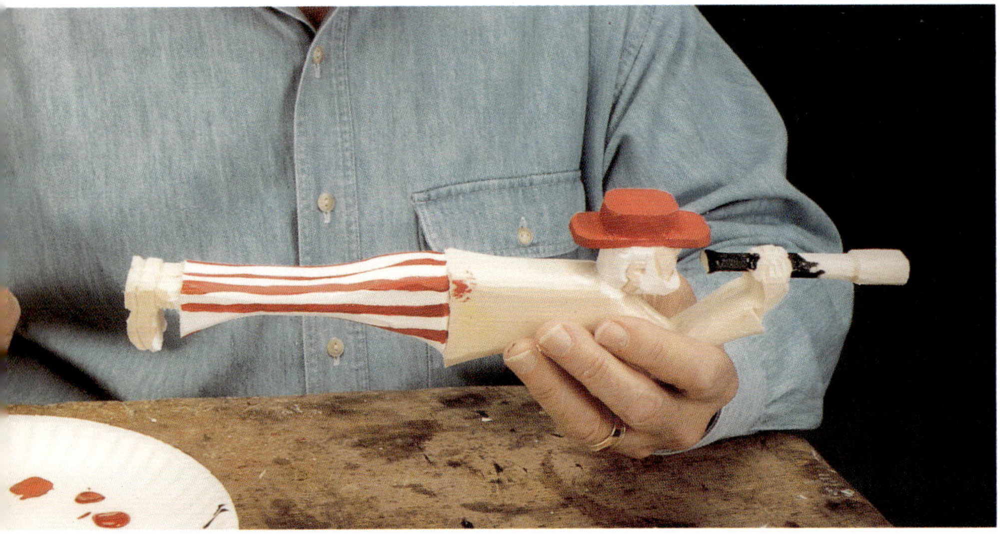

I've decided, with my photographer Dawn's encouragement, to make the Summertime figure an Uncle Sam. You decide what you would like to do. I painted the trousers white with red stripes, the hat red, beard and hair white, and the telescope black.

Uncle Sam's face. Notice that one eye is closed, because you can't look at a telescope with both eyes at the same time. Paint just a little black line and a black dot for the open eye. I used Santa's Flesh for the face, painted in a small red line for the mouth, and added eyebrows.

Paint the jacket navy blue.

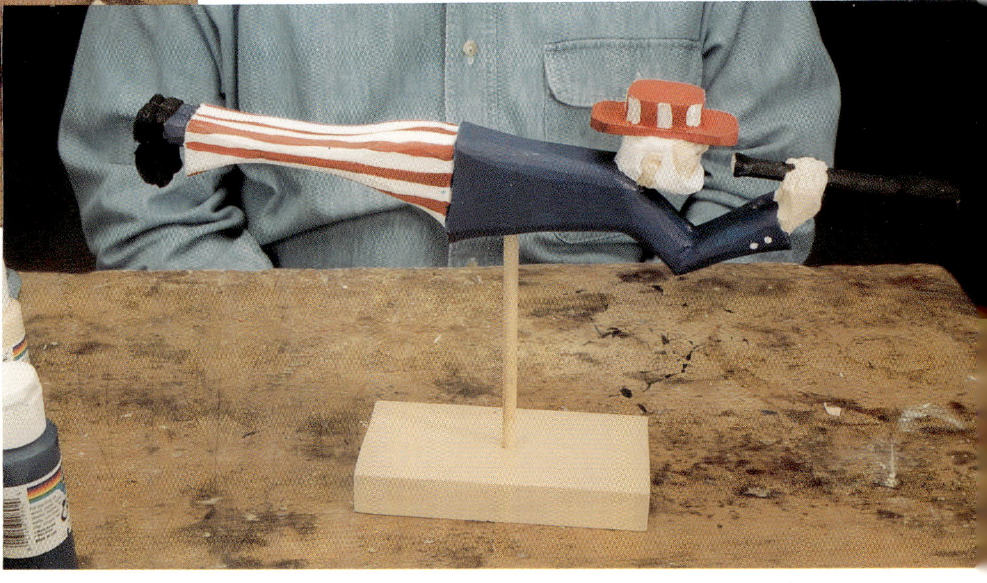

Socks are painted blue, shoes black, white stripes on the hat.

Antiquing

Those of you who are familiar with my other methods of antiquing know that Griffin shoe polish is no longer available. If you are using Briwax and like the results, continue to use it. The method I am going to tell you about here is the method used by my friend Claude Bolton, cowboy carver extraordinaire.

Mix boiled linseed oil and turpentine or turpenoid half and half. Add a dab of burnt umber oil paint and shake. If you prefer a darker finish add more umber.

After your carving is painted and dry, paint on the mixture. After this dries, put a coat of Flecto brand Varathane diamond finish clear satin. The Varathane will protect as well as give a nice finish to your work.

I put my mixture in a covered (empty of course) mayo jar. Shake it before each use and it will last for a long time. I still prefer Ceramcoat acrylic paint from Delta Technical Coatings, Inc. I am a paint junkie and am fascinated by all the colors available. I have paint I've had for ten years and it still works fine.

The Gallery

RANSOM
'97

WITCH
PARKING
ONLY
OTHERS WILL BE
TOAD!

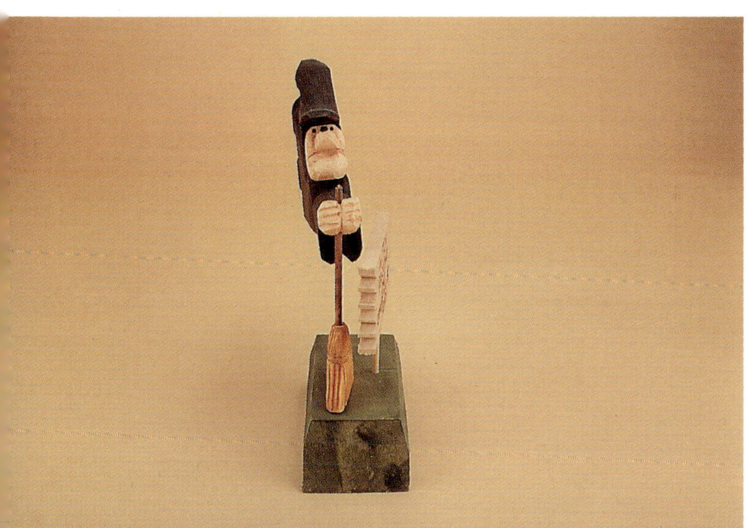

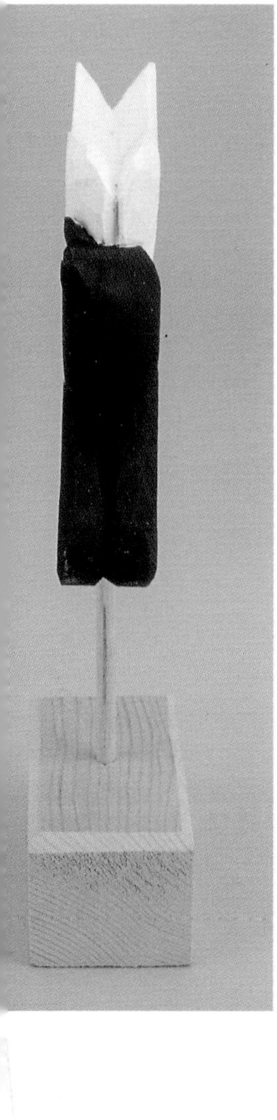

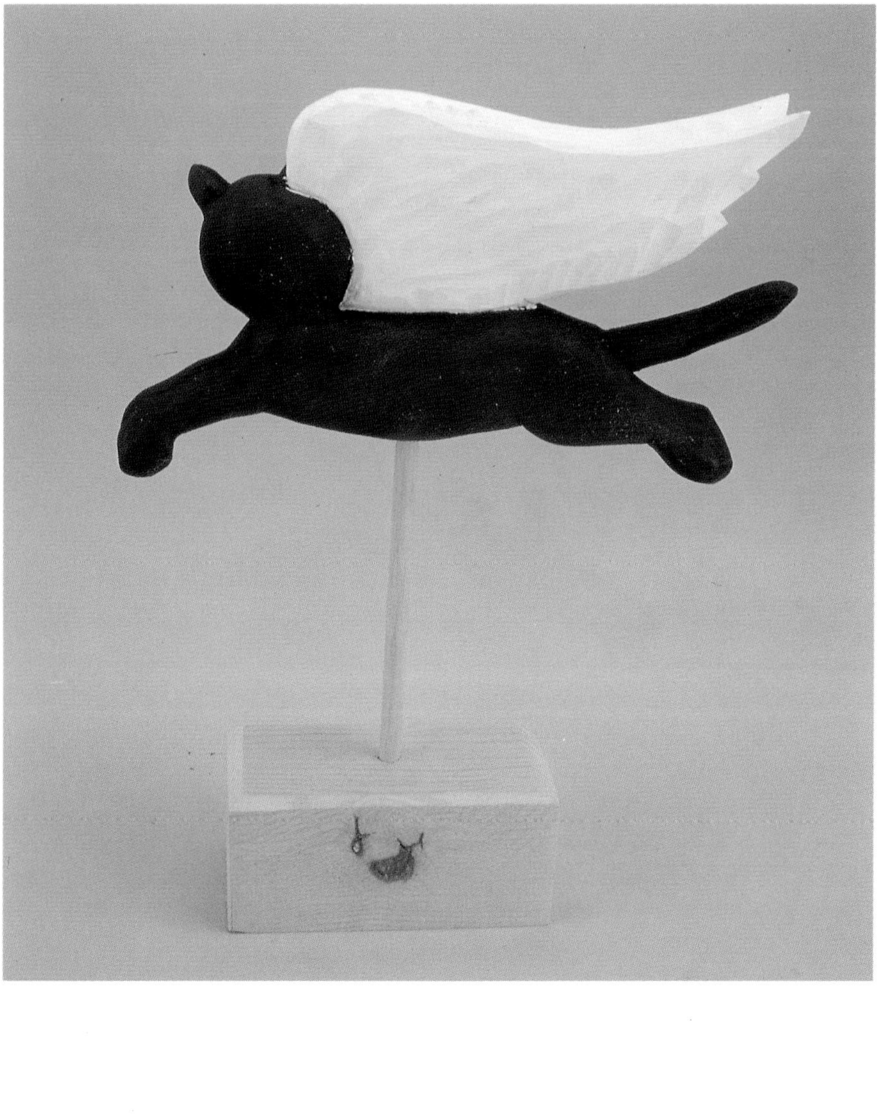

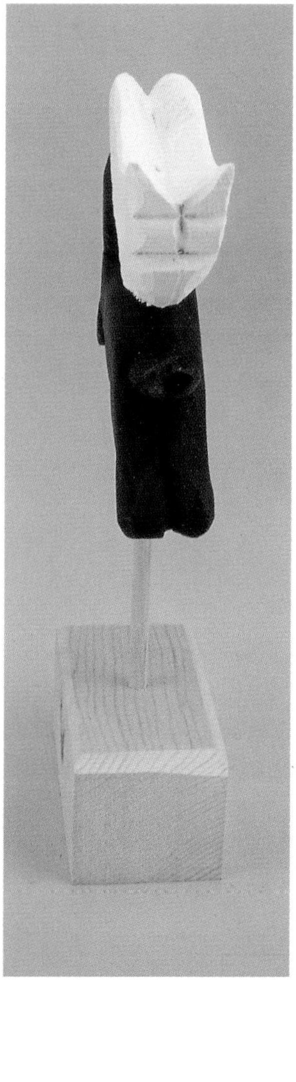

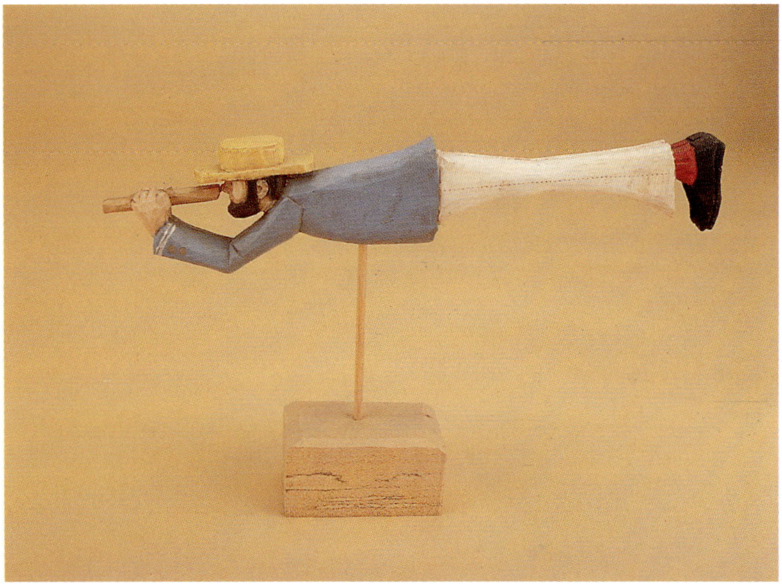

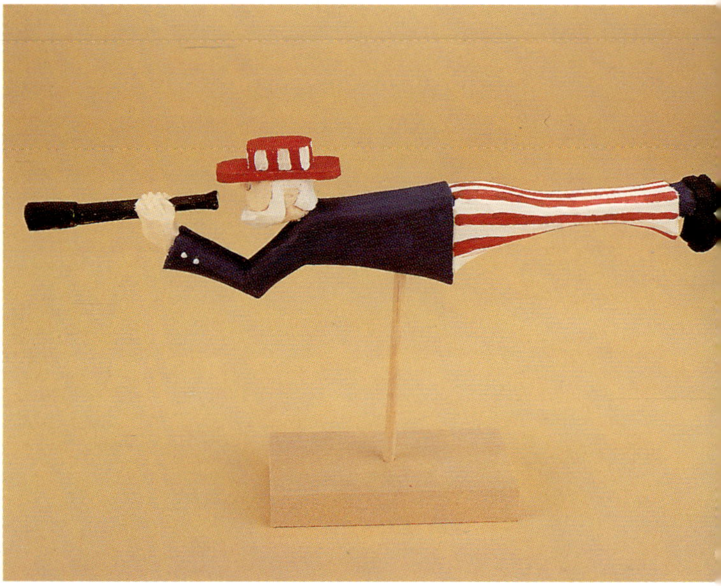